TRIing TIMES

Stories of Tragedy and Triumph from Triathletes Around the World

By Valerie Haller and
Personal Power Press

TRIing TIMES

Stories of Tragedy and Triumph from Triathletes
Around the World

© 2020 by Valerie Haller and Personal Power Press

Library of Congress Control Number: 2020936301

ISBN: 978-0-9772321-1-6

Printed in the United States of America

Personal Power Press, Inc.

Bay City, MI 48706

Cover Design

Parker Haller - parkerhaller72@gmail.com

Table of Contents

www.tommyzphotos.com

Foreword

Katie Zaferes

As a professional triathlete and the 2019 International Triathlon Union (ITU) World Champion, an Olympian and Super League Champion, I have moved up the ranks since my recruitment following college. I too have experienced some TRI-ing times. One of my major goals in 2019 was to qualify for the 2020 Olympics at the first opportunity, the Tokyo Test event in August. Leading into the race I was in an awesome place both physically and mentally. I felt calm and ready.

The race started in typical fashion for me. I came out of the water as usual, in the front third of the pack, which put me in the lead group on the bike. During the second lap, I made a silly mistake. I looked back to offer words of encouragement to our breakaway group. In doing so I swerved my bike into a barrier, slid and crashed. In a fraction of a second I was laying on the pavement. I could feel cuts in my mouth and a faint taste of blood. Groups were cycling past me while blood was dripping from my face. I was standing at the roadside, dazed and confused, assessing my bike and considering a simple wheel change to continue the race. But it turned out I had done more damage and was unable to continue. Race officials escorted me off the course and immediately transported me to the hospital by ambulance.

I lay in the back of the ambulance, distraught. I made a mistake that could cost me my Olympic qualification. And possibly my World Championship at the Grand Final in Lausanne, Switzerland in just two weeks. I was sad that despite all my hard work and dedication I may not meet my goal. I broke my nose and received twenty-three stitches in my mouth. I am so thankful for the support of so many people at the race — the medical staff at the hospital, fellow competitors and friends showing concern and support from afar, and of course my husband Tommy. They all helped me heal, recover and regain my race resolve.

After leaving Tokyo and heading to our Pre-Grand Final camp in Thonon-les-Bains, France, I had to take it day by day. A key component to my athletic career, in college and as a pro, has been to train my brain as much as my body. I knew that my body could handle what my mind could manage. So, I put my mind to work. I made specific goals for each day and kept my focus on what I could do in preparation for Lausanne. I embraced both the good and the bad days, knowing that progress is not always linear. I remained confident in myself and in all the training that I put in — not just in 2019 — but in all the years since I started triathlon. I celebrated each small victory: swimming with both arms, the fact that my stitches were inside my mouth so I could put my face in the water and swim, and my facial injuries had no impact on my biking or running.

My sports psychologist helped me reframe my mental strategies to be specific to preparing for the Grand Final, considering the circumstances. One of my main goals in Lausanne was just getting around the bike course safely. This was always something that I wanted, but not usually something that ended up on my pre-race goal list. I kept my focus on my strengths. I was grateful for the time I had in the water even though my swim practice was limited because of the facial injuries. I was strong on the bike, but my technical confidence was waning. Yet I knew that when it was time to run, I would be alright.

On the day of the race I was scared, nervous and uncertain how the race would unfold. I decided to focus on my strength in each discipline, one at a time. The swim went smoothly. I stayed in a safe position around the buoys to protect my face from being bumped and I pulled hard to keep pace in the straights. As I exited the water, I felt myself relax into the flow. On the bike, if a gap formed from being technically conservative, I used my strength on the hills and the straights to regain position. I became more comfortable with each corner.

Then it was time to run. To claim the World Title, I had to finish in the top 13. I didn't want the crash in Tokyo to define me and I needed to prove that I was the same athlete as before. I wanted to win. I was fortunate that although I sustained injuries, I was able to walk away from the crash, continue training, and successfully complete my next race. I won the race that day and became the 2019 ITU World Champion.

My fellow triathletes' personal journeys featured in *TRIing Times* present many themes that resonate with me. I am amazed and inspired by each person's ability to persevere through their hardships, demonstrating their strength to overcome. I appreciate the description from Jennifer Klause, "The most precious part about these games is not the athletic competitions, but rather the relationships you build with people from all over the world. All of whom have gone through something similar that you have gone through, yet each story is unique and beautiful." That is what I see in *TRIing Times*. The variety of individual stories provides opportunities for the reader to connect in their own personal way. There is comfort in knowing that others have felt the way we have. Our feelings are justified, and we are not alone.

I can sense the mental fortitude and strength within each of the authors. I appreciate the candidness of the struggle, the truth that sometimes terrible, unexpected, scary, and difficult things happen in life. Each story demonstrates both the fragility of life, and the strong will of the individual athlete to work through those moments. And to prove there is a way to navigate through them. I realize the important role that community often plays in overcoming difficult times, whether it be family, friends, sports psychologists, coaches, teammates, medical staff, or race personnel.

In my own experience, I have made very few changes with my physical training. However, I have had to work on a strong mindset that is adaptable and ready for whatever unexpected events arise. In the moments where I have been tested, I have learned the most about my inner self, which is a universal theme in *TRIing Times*.

Introduction

Thomas Haller

Every triathlete in the race was on the bike course. The transition area looked bare. The air was filled with anticipation as the spectators began to gather at the bike-in entrance. All eyes were glaring down the road to a corner that sent the athletes down the gauntlet to the transition area. We waited.

The cool morning air was beginning to give way to a gentle warming as the sun radiated through the trees. Then someone shouted, "Biker up!" The crowd burst into chatter as folks jockeyed for a better view. The spec in the distance quickly took shape, a lone rider tightly tucked onto the aerobars and bearing down on the pedals. A few began to murmur, "Who is it?" Only a couple blocks remained, and all would have the answer.

Clanging cow bells and screeching horns filled the air as the biker slipped each foot out of the bike shoe and placed each bare foot on top of the shoe. Still pedaling hard with a block to go, I turned to the guy standing next to me and exclaimed, "That's my wife!"

I watched Valerie swing her leg around the saddle and gently balance on one side of the bike. She slowed enough to jump from the bike and continued running with her right hand holding the saddle. I looked over her shoulder and saw no one. As she passed, I shouted, "Valerie, you're first off the bike! No one is right behind you." I pushed my stopwatch and started time to the next athlete. I kept one eye on the road and one on Valerie, watching her rack her bike, slip on her running shoes and head out of transition.

I waited for the next biker to reach transition, marked the time on my watch and looked at the back of the person's left leg. "Damn," I said under my breath as I headed for the run course. I took a shortcut through a back alley and behind a row of houses to reach the run course with a little over two miles to go. Valerie was moving towards me at a steady pace. As she approached, I shouted, "You were four minutes up on the second-place biker. She's twenty-two and a runner." Valerie huffed passed and I shouted, "You've got this!"

I took the short cuts back and met Valerie crossing the finishing line. After only four years competing in triathlons, she reached the podium that day. First overall — one minute, twenty seconds ahead of the second-place finisher.

Five years later, on a hot April day in St. Petersburg, Florida, nearly four thousand triathletes gathered to compete. I just finished my race and exited the area as quickly as possible. I cut across the street and ran down the road to wait for Valerie on the run course. I picked a spot where I could shout a few words of encouragement as she ran by and still make it back to see her cross the finish line. She huffed passed (in usual fashion) and I shouted, "You've got this!" I felt a lump in my throat and started to cry. I jogged back to the finish line and met Valerie as she crossed. We embraced each other and stood crying together.

Eight weeks prior to the race in St. Pete's, Valerie completed treatment for breast cancer. Her motivational declaration through surgery and the subsequent treatment was, "I've got this." Her mental therapy was writing about her feelings, fears, and expectations as she went through the process of ridding herself of cancer.

As the CEO of an independent publishing company, I encouraged Valerie to share her story in a published book to help others find their motivational voice in the face of personal struggles. She agreed only if we could provide the same opportunity for other triathletes who also had a powerful message to convey. Out of that came the birth of *TRIing Times*.

This book you hold in your hands is a collection of life-stories from triathletes around the world. Professional and retired elite triathletes, long-course IRONMAN® triathletes, age-group world and national triathlon competitors, and age-group local triathlon competitors have come together to lend their inspiring voices. What you will find in these stories is a unique outlook on life that has enabled each contributing author to face their fear, overcome a painful or tragic experience, regain a sense of purpose, and triumph over the tragedy. They found an avenue of hope, tranquility, motivation, and renewed passion in the wake of their personal tragedy.

Through these stories we hope to inspire others from all walks of life who have experienced heartbreak, illness, catastrophe, or devastation and help them turn their pain into power. Our desire is that within these pages, you will find a part of yourself that enables you to keep going in trying times.

"Aspire to inspire before you expire."

~ Unknown

I've Got This!

Valerie Haller

I'm 52 years old and in the best shape of my adult life. I just finished racing in Australia representing my country on Team USA in the ITU Finals. The venue was beautiful; the city of Gold Coast gleamed in the sunshine. It was paradise. I was finally happy in my own skin. I was strong, healthy, and mentally pleased with my life. The race was over and my husband, Tom and I were getting ready for a day of sightseeing. While getting dressed I felt a little lump on my breast. I shrugged it off in my mind knowing that this was not unusual as my cycle was near. I got confirmation from Tom — he could feel something too. Since there was no pain, we agreed to monitor things from there.

We returned to our normal lives. Tri season was over and what a season it had been. I'd crashed my bike in Toronto resulting in a broken wrist only 10 weeks before Australia. I missed Nationals in

Cleveland. I was back to teaching Kindergarten. You know the ABCs, counting to 100, singing and playing. But that little lump remained — no change in size and still no pain. I have no history of breast cancer in my family. I was sure it was just a cyst that needed to be addressed. I made an appointment with the OB and I was put through the paces. Just to cover the bases, they scheduled a mammogram and a biopsy. I had been through that once before and the results were benign.

Tom and I met with the doctor. It's an odd experience when you hear your doctor say, "I'm sorry Valerie, the results of the biopsy show Stage 1 cancer cells." Tom was sitting next to me. He slid his hand underneath mine and squeezed it gently. Dr. Bays' voice continued but all I heard was the muffled voice from the *Peanuts* cartoon, "Wa-waa-whaa-whaa-wa." Tears flowed down my cheeks. I managed a breath and asked my burning question: "What about training?" A puzzled look came across the doctor's face. "What training?" she asked. I looked pleadingly at Tom. He filled in the blanks for me as I sobbed quietly. He explained that I was a triathlete and had just competed in Australia. I had plans to qualify for Worlds in Edmonton.

Dr. Bays took a deep breath and replied, "I understand, my husband is a triathlete too." She asked about my training plans and my next scheduled race. Tom rattled off a brief outline of the plan and specified the next race, "The St. Anthony's TRI in St. Petersburg, Florida at the end of April." The look on her face indicated that she knew and understood the drive toward my goal. I told her I wanted to have the surgery ASAP and she agreed. A minute of silence filled the air. Dr. Bays whispered something to her nurse and the nurse nodded in agreement. Then the doctor said, "I'm out of the hospital on Christmas vacation for the next two weeks." She paused and with a determined look on her face said, "Valerie, I want you to keep that April race as your goal. I will schedule only one surgery during my break — yours."

On January 2, 2019 the lumpectomy was performed. The graciousness of Dr. Bays helped me keep to my goal by putting the surgery behind me.

Back home Tom rearranged our bedroom for my healing. I had a recliner, a computer table within reach, a mini fridge, a large screen TV and all the warmest blankets. My mother came home from Florida to take care of me. She arrived at our house promptly the day after surgery at 8:00 am to take her first shift of post-surgery care. The bedroom was empty. She started making phone calls fearing that I had an issue and was back in the hospital. She called my cell and I answered in a pleasant, upbeat voice.

She asked, "Where are you?"

"I'm at the fitness center walking on the treadmill," I replied.

She breathed a sigh of relief and I'm sure rolled her eyes. I followed the doctor's orders, but I didn't stay down. Nobody told me I couldn't walk and maybe jog a little here and there. I was prescribed one month of healing with ample opportunities for light treadmill walking and stationary biking before the next step. My mom's time as my "recovery nurse" was extremely easy.

Radiation was the next step in my cancer treatment. At the initial visit to the radiation center, the nurse went through my health history. My blood pressure was 108/65 and my heart rate was 52. She also asked me pages and pages of questions, "Do you have this... Do you have that... Have you ever...?"

I answered, "No, no, no, no, no," to everything.

At the end the nurse exclaimed, "You are the healthiest person I know."

I replied, "And I have cancer." She took in a deep breath as that settled in the room.

My radiation treatment was scheduled for each day after school throughout the month of February. Tom wanted to take me to those appointments, but I told him I wanted to do it myself. I drove directly from school to the appointment and home afterwards each day. My mantra had become, "I've got this."

I elected to do what is called the breath-hold method for radiation. I would take in a deep breath to use the lungs to raise the breast and position it as far away from the heart as possible. On my first visit for treatment I was in position. Through the speaker system the technician told me to take in a deep breath and hold. I heard the machine whirl, click and stop. There was a long pause, then the technician said, "Oh, you can breathe now." This was repeated several times. At the completion the technician came into the room, she asked, "Are you an athlete? You can hold your breath for a long time. Sorry, I forgot to tell you to breathe after the first one."

I wasn't allowed to swim during radiation. The pool chemicals can be very harsh on fragile radiated skin. I was still running and biking. Running in Michigan in the winter is hit and miss, well mostly miss. Weather didn't cooperate with my training, but I went out after treatments anyway. The radiation techs asked if I was experiencing fatigue, and I was. They asked what that meant to me. I told them that I didn't feel like running three miles after treatment, but I was doing it anyway. They were confused. Typically, patients were not working full time during treatments and they were certainly not doing any form of exercise, let alone training for a triathlon. I worked full time and I trained daily. I was not going to be defined by my diagnosis. I continued to train on the bike trainer in the basement. Tom even rigged up a support system for me to do the "rollers" in the basement. I wasn't confident in my ability to stay on the rollers, so this gave me support. I kept repeating, "I've got this!"

Each month seemed to bring its challenges with the new protocols of my treatment. In March I started taking a daily dose of Tamoxifen to block the estrogen in my system and starve any future cancer cells. That would be the protocol for the next ten years. As I took the first dose, I started to cry, gagged and coughed it up. My last bit of refusal before submitting. Tom held my hand as I choked down that first pill. I still have an occasional issue with swallowing that pill.

I continued to train. My focus was on the April race. My "prove it to myself" race. My "I've got this!" race. As the days drew closer, I questioned myself, "Can I compete? Am I healthy enough? Am I strong enough?" I posed these questions to my husband. He would just smile and say, "You've got this."

Tom and I flew to Florida. It would be our first open water swim of the year and our first outdoor bike of the year. The weather was beautiful. We met up with a few Michigan teammates (Team ATP) who were also participating in the race and did a course preview. We noted trouble spots on the bike course and swam with the group in the swim preview.

Then it was finally race day. I didn't sleep much the night before. I spent most of the night chasing away negative thoughts with, "I've got this." I was as ready as I could be. The swim was smooth especially with it being my first open water swim of the season. The bike was great! I love snuggling onto the aerobars and letting it rip. The run was a different story. I struggled in the heat and my legs were heavy, like lead. I had to look down at my feet several times to see if they were coming up off the pavement. I drudged on, coaxing my legs with every step, "Come on legs, you've got this." Tom was at the finish. I fell into his arms and whimpered, "I've got this." He held me tight and said, "Yes you do. Yes, you do!"

Our race calendar for the rest of 2019 remained full. We continued to train and race. I competed in three aquathons (swim/run) placing second female overall for the series and then four triathlons, where I qualified for USA Triathlon (USAT) Nationals. I continued to struggle with my run. My run performance did not even compare to my early years in triathlon. Radiation had affected my entire body. I continued to train through the summer and into the fall and participated in the USAT Nationals in Cleveland in August and the Draft Legal Nationals in Arizona in November.

I missed making Team USA by three spots. My performance was just out of qualifying range.

I will continue to train. I will continue to drive the free radicals from radiation out of my system. I will continue to get stronger and push harder. I will continue. Cancer won't define me.

What is still confusing to me is the how. How did this happen when I was doing everything right? I never "felt" sick. But I had sickness in me. I'll never know the how or the why. But what I do know is this — I have my focus, I have my people, I have my goals, I have my determination. And now, I have a daily ritual. Each morning I begin my day by looking in the mirror and saying out loud, "I've got this!"

Remember to look in the mirror. That's your competition!

Photo by Wendy Andrews

Ripped Until I Die

Lauren Jensen McGinnis

This story cannot be told without recognition of my friend, one rare soul, Jeff Littmann. Everyone called him 'Littmann' as it seemed appropriate to call an athlete by his last name. He was a man of few words, but the words he spoke highlighted his thoughtfulness, intelligence and kind heart. In his thoughtfulness, he approached everything and everyone with a steadiness of character. In his kindness, he gave everyone the benefit of the doubt. While he had no biological children of his own, Littmann had paternal strength that naturally attracted people to him.

Not only did Littmann lead the pack on the group bike rides, but he also successfully led the various businesses that he owned. As a former bodybuilder turned cyclist, Littmann was a specimen of pure muscle. Powerful tattoos adorned his body including a large, colorful tiger. When someone told him that this tiger tattoo would 'look ridiculous' as he aged, Littmann's response was simple. And unfortunately, as fate would have it, truthful: "I will be ripped until I die!"

It was October 1, 2010. Having competed as an Elite/Pro Triathlete in IRONMAN® Wisconsin weeks earlier, I was enjoying a well-earned off-season. Littmann and I set out for a casual ride and we rolled down the road chatting. Littmann shared with me his love for his new wife Kelly, and how amazing his life had become. We discussed our plans to partner and to help me make my Tri Faster Coaching business more successful. That was Littmann: he was a true giver who was driven to help others. We enjoyed the sunshine, the ride, and I always enjoyed hearing Littmann speak from his heart. Life was good. As we rode together sharing and making plans, I felt so ALIVE!

It was a flat road and I was riding in the shoulder. In his protective manner, Littmann rode one-half of a bike length back, slightly left of the white shoulder line. As we traveled along talking, the sound of his warm-hearted voice was suddenly replaced by a horrific BANG! Catapulted through the air, I landed 25-feet away. I bounced another 10 feet, bike still attached by my bike shoes, with no recognition of what happened.

I looked around and thought – "What happened? And where the Hell is Littmann?"

Then I saw it. A scene that I will always carry, every day: a few hundred yards up the road, a car halfway in the shoulder and a body lying on the ground. Unaware of my injuries, powered by ten times my race-level adrenaline, I ran to Littmann.

As I gazed down at him, my former training as a Lifeguard Instructor kicked in. He was breathing, but he was unconscious, bleeding from his skull, ears and nose which suggested a very serious head injury. I told the driver, who was calling 911, to request for Flight for Life. As I monitored Littmann, I prayed! I am one of the world's biggest optimists, but at that moment my optimism did not prevail. I called my husband, Todd, from the side of the road. I told him what happened, and that I was not sure that Jeff was going to make it. I distinctly remember calling him Jeff, not Littmann.

Perhaps the name Jeff was more human to me than the invincible Littmann.

While it felt like an eternity, emergency personnel quickly arrived, and Flight for Life soon followed. As I scanned the accident scene, I realized that Jeff had ended up on the windshield of the car. Meanwhile his bike was dragged underneath, crumpled up like a miniature circus-clown bike. My strong friend had been carried on the car's windshield down the road, before the car stopped and he rolled off onto the street. It could have been a shared fate, but the car hit the back of my bike and sent me flying instead. I am only alive today because the car never hit my body, which certainly would have pulverized all 120 pounds of me.

Jeff was airlifted to the Trauma Center. I was walking around with no sign of injury other than severe road rash. While being interviewed by the emergency personnel, I realized that I could not lift my left arm. As a Physical Therapist, I knew what that meant and calmly said, "I may have broken my collarbone." Then there was a flurry of activity around me. I was fit into a cervical collar, strapped to a backboard and loaded into an ambulance. They wanted to take me to the nearest hospital, but I refused. I needed to be near Jeff, and I insisted that they take me to the same hospital. Finally they agreed, and they doped me up with morphine noting that "it's going to be a bumpy ride." I swear they hit every pothole on purpose out of spite for having to drive me an extra 20 miles.

The Emergency Room visit was a blur. I remember being badgered by the police officer who interviewed me while he spewed his opinion that cyclists should never ride on the road. Maybe that is what made me puke. Or maybe it was the morphine, or perhaps it was from my head and neck that had been rattled from the impact.

I was released hours later and went to the family ICU waiting room where many had gathered in support of Jeff. My friend who was a physician pulled me aside and gently told me, "Lauren, you need to prepare yourself. It is unlikely that he is going to make it." This bleak outlook was confirmed when I visited him in the ICU the next day. He was still unconscious, looking like an Oompa Loompa from the steroids.

I knew what would transpire. I cried.

A few nights later as I rested in the recliner at home, I was bolted awake by a dream. I saw a white spirit lift from Jeff's body and ascend into the heavens. I knew that God had taken his soul. Later I would learn that moments before I had that dream, Jeff's stepson Michael also had a dream where Jeff came to him and requested him to "Let me go." Michael told Kelly about the dream, and together they made the difficult decision to take Jeff off life support and honored his wishes to be an organ donor. Jeff left this world at the young age of 56. I think about the providence of this dream often, as it cultivated my spirituality far more than attending eight years of Catholic school ever did.

Jeff's funeral was a testament to the many lives he impacted. There were easily 4,000 people in attendance and the visitation line went out of the church, down the block and around the corner. I was still in shock and I was further numbed by the pain meds. Yet I still remember staring at the box that contained Jeff's ashes. I remember the profound contradiction: someone with an influence that was bigger than life, reduced to the contents of that tiny box of ashes. I also remember the many well-meaning but completely asinine things that people said to me. One comment that really irked me was, *"You were spared because you still have things to give to this world."* That discounted Jeff and all that he had left to give to the world as well, but the inattentive driver stole that opportunity from him. The second statement that made me cringe was, *"I am glad you are okay!"*

I was ALIVE — but in no way was I okay.

A few short weeks before the accident I had completed a hilly Ironman (2.4-mile swim, a 112-mile bike ride, and a 26.2-mile run) in just over 10 hours. Now I was living out of a recliner and my "exercise" was walking 30 feet to the bathroom. One morning I got dizzy on the bathroom trek and took a rest on the kitchen floor. Todd had to coax me back to the recliner before our son David saw me there.

David had just turned nine, and in many ways, he was a typical young boy full of energy and wonder. In other ways he was not typical. As an only child, David was much better at communicating with adults than with his peers, and we enjoyed a comfortable and close relationship. He was, and still is, a bright young man who easily makes logical connections between things.

Even more profound than David's natural intellect, is his capacity for immense empathy. The combination of his ability to draw quick conclusions combined with his deep capacity to feel for my situation, led to some significant struggles for David. For some time, the parental/child roles seemed to have been turned upside down and his worry for my well-being created palpable anxiety for David.

I was not doing much better emotionally than David. I was diagnosed with PTSD (Post Traumatic Stress Disorder) and anything that sounded like a loud bang — a cabinet door slamming or a loud knock on the door, sent me into a tear-filled panic. My heart rate was consistently elevated, and I struggled to sleep. The nightmares of the accident scene or dreams of getting hit haunted me every night. I felt powerless, vulnerable, and unsafe — even in the recliner. It was many months before I could drive on the freeway. I feared being rear-ended. Even with two years of therapy, there are still remnants of PTSD when I am tailgated in my vehicle or when I hear loud sounds.

As sorrowful as the driver Kyle was at the accident scene, that was the only time we ever spoke. It's unfortunate that our society 'fixes' tragedies through insurance companies and attorneys instead of via open and reparative communication. The driver claimed that the morning sun blinded him, so he never saw us — an idea that one of the emergency personnel suggested at the accident scene.

He also lied. He claimed that he was wearing sunglasses and that he was not speeding. The scene's evidence showed that he was driving over the speed limit and drove his car halfway into the shoulder. If he were truly blinded by the sun, then why wouldn't he have slowed down? I have 100 questions that will never be answered. Kyle lawyered up, never apologized, and put his own interests in front of doing the right thing.

I was appalled when the detective defended the driver. Instead of getting my side of the story, he spent most of the meeting telling me to go easy on Kyle: *He is a young guy with a new baby.* Really!?! What about Jeff who we will never see again? What about the abrupt and unplanned end to my career as an Elite Athlete? What about my numerous injuries and the fact that I had not slept a single night since the accident? In the end, Kyle received two tickets for failure to yield to a cyclist. I was beyond pissed.

Between the PTSD and my anger with Kyle, I was banged up emotionally, but the injuries to my body were equally challenging. Initially, I thought that the primary injury was the broken collarbone. I spent 21 weeks with horrific bone and nerve pain, visiting the orthopedic surgeon frequently. I think that I shouted "FiretrUCK" in his office just about every visit when I learned that it was not healing. I begged for the surgery. Perhaps tired of my F-bombs, the surgeon granted me the surgery before the standard 26-weeks. Post-surgery the bone still did not heal, so I was sent for a battery of tests and injections until the Vitamin D deficiency was identified and addressed. I also shouted "FiretrUCK" at physical therapy as the painful muscle tightness and nerve impingements related to my injuries were addressed.

Discovering the depth of my injuries was like peeling an onion: as each surface injury began to heal, I learned more about other ailments. As the collarbone healed, I was able to do more training, and layer-by-layer I learned the true extent of my brokenness. Following surgery, I developed a nearly frozen shoulder. I had herniated several vertebrae in my neck that made cycling in the aero position unbearable. Then I discovered my most significant injury: the accident tore my Sacro-Iliac (SI) joint wide open. The physician told me that it was either the worst SI tear he had ever seen, or perhaps I was tied with a patient who had been thrown from a horse. As competitive as I am, having the 'Most Injured SI Joint' was one contest that I did not want to win. There were many weeks when I had as many as nine medical appointments, a schedule that was very disruptive to my life and to my family's. It took two years of injections and endless physical therapy sessions, plus daily exercises from my own knowledge of physical therapy to stabilize my movements.

Despite all these emotional and physical challenges, it was with stubborn confidence that I took out a Pro/Elite racing license in 2011. My friend, Brent, spent hours getting me a bike fit much less aerodynamic than I used to ride, but one that I could tolerate. Another friend, Sheryl, got me back riding on the road for the first time. There were many rides where I ended up in a panic along the side of the road because a motorcycle rumbled past me or something else triggered my PTSD. My body was fragmented, and my fitness was poor, but my desire was strong. I soaked up every bit of improvement as encouragement to sustain me in my fight back each day. I had an entire *Humpty Dumpty Team* who put me back together again, and I will be forever grateful to them for helping me not only to live, but to be ALIVE.

I did my best to keep my optimism: believing with every broken ounce of myself that I would race again as an Elite/Pro Triathlete. It was something that I had done for 17 years and it was something that made me feel ALIVE! Over the years I had raced at this high level while I worked full time, attended physical therapy school, raised a child, and eventually while I built a successful coaching career. Racing was in my blood and I loved everything about it from the rigorous training, to the hours spent outside, to the shared experience with friends, to the race adrenaline. My resting heart rate was about 40 bpm, yet I could elevate it to 140 bpm at the starting line of a race, just standing there not moving. That is when I felt MOST ALIVE, when I was racing and when I was in *The Zone* - mindful of my breathing and my every movement.

Kyle had stolen Jeff from us, but I refused to allow him to steal from me what made me feel so ALIVE. I regrouped. I healed. I trained hard. I learned how to use my body again. I gave it my all. But I sucked! I very slowly accepted that my long race days and racing on an Elite Level were behind me. Once again, I cried, for Jeff, but also for myself.

It is quite common for individuals who have gone through a life-changing event to scrutinize their life. The physical re-invention was only the tip of the iceberg. My marriage of 22 years ended in divorce in January of 2015. That was something that required more therapy, both individual as well as couples counselling. Even though we were a mismatched couple, my Catholic upbringing along with my *never-quit* mentality created a depth of guilt around what I perceived as a "failed marriage". Looking back after a few years of working our way through, I believe that all three of us — Todd, David and I — are happier.

Far before I forgave myself for divorcing, I had an emotional breakthrough by deciding to forgive Kyle. Realizing that there is a difference between forgiveness and reconciliation helped me to accept that I would never receive an apology from him. We would never have the chance to reconcile because the insurance companies communicated for us. However, forgiving him allowed me to move forward and embrace what was then my new normal.

Slowly I realized that a return to Age Group racing would allow me to continue to compete on a level that was healthy for my body. I could feel ALIVE, but without toppling over the delicate balance that my body had become. Initially I raced Olympic Distance events that took over two hours to complete. Over time I realized and accepted that even that was too much, and I settled on sprint races that took a little over an hour.

In my return to the Age Group ranks, luck was on my side. My home city of Milwaukee hosted the USAT Age Group National Championships from 2013-2015. This gave me a chance to race the best Age Groupers right in my backyard. Each year I set the goal of winning a National Championship. I came close, settling for two Silver Medals and one Bronze Medal. In addition, the ITU World Championships were held nearby in Chicago, and I competed there with vigor bringing home the Silver Medal. I loved competitive racing, although being the bridesmaid but never the bride made me hungry for more.

Using my knowledge as a Physical Therapist and triathlon coach, I tweaked my training and increased the emphasis on strength training and short but intense intervals. I would never be as fast as I was before the accident, but little by little I was improving despite getting older. A breakthrough happened and I captured my first USAT Sprint Triathlon Age Group National Champion Title in 2016 and repeated it in 2017. I accepted the invitation to represent Team USA at the ITU Sprint Triathlon World Championships in 2018 in Australia. After finishing second at the ITU World Championships in 2015, I set the bold goal of winning the Gold Medal at the World's Championship in 2018.

I had 13 months to prepare which was ample time. But in November 2017, I unfortunately tore the meniscus in my right knee and needed surgery, rehab and a hiatus from training. I was just getting back into good shape in May 2018 when I sprained my ankle badly enough to end up in a boot, another setback to my training. Through these setbacks my optimism ruled, and I never gave up on my goal of becoming a World Champion. I was no stranger to overcoming obstacles, so when I could not physically train, I worked on my mental preparation.

My life was blessed, and a friendship turned romantic — Dan and I were married in April 2018. I could not have asked for a better partner and supporter. Race day came and I woke up with a quiet confidence. I knew it was my race to lose. Since my surgeon had put me on a weekly budget of 12 miles of running, I knew I had to lead off the bike. I brought the mental game to race day and it went very much like the hundreds of times I had visualized it. I was second out of the water in my division, but over a minute off the lead. I biked HARD and I felt amazing! I had visualized the course so many times that I seemed to fly through the technical sections. When I got off the bike, Dan was standing in the perfect place to shout, "You are in the lead!" I almost came to a stop as I shouted back, "Really?!" Then I ran like a scared rabbit for the 5K run. I feel like I did not exhale until I closed in on the finish line to hear, "Here comes the World Champion in the 50-54 division – Lauren Jensen McGinnis!"

I cried again, but that time it was very happy tears.

You were spared because you still have things to give to this world: a statement that still annoys me, but also challenges me. The desire to help others has always been in me, although the accident created an urgency to up the ante. Soon after the accident, I created and hosted the Tri Faster Pedal for the Food Pantry charity event. With the help of many volunteers we raised over $20,000 along with countless food donations during five years of running the event.

In 2012, I began coaching Team Phoenix, an innovative program that helps female cancer survivors train for their first triathlon. Over a seven-year period I had the honor of coaching more than 250 women in all age groups through their training and racing transformation. While I will never understand exactly what cancer survivors have been through, the accident did help me understand elements of their journey — looking death in the face and surviving, countless medical pokes and prods, but most importantly reinventing themselves. The places where they have scars are now the strongest parts of their constitution. Many of these women have continued to train under my guidance through Tri Faster and will be representing Team USA at the 2020 Aquathon World Championships — their accomplishments are truly amazing!

This past year, I teamed up with my son as well as some friends and created a non-profit group called Making Waves Milwaukee. Our mission is to teach adults to swim, especially those who have a medical diagnosis that would benefit from swimming. We allow anyone with financial need to attend free of charge thanks to a grant from the USMS Swimming Saves Lives Foundation. The most meaningful part of this program is to help others alongside David — to see my son embrace the desire to make a difference in the world. It is the best legacy I could ever hope to create.

Jeff Littmann is no longer here leading the way, but his strength can still be felt. I AM ALIVE, and I have the opportunity to emulate his giving spirit and to build on the many lessons that his life and death taught me. I may or may not be "ripped until I die," but I plan to continually find new ways to follow in Littmann's footsteps and to make a positive difference in our world.

Big thanks to my friend Hillary Bowser for helping me tell my story.

Death to Victory in 90 Days

Edward Marx

My entry into multi-sport may be a little atypical. I started racing to encourage our oldest son to become fit. Despite fit parents, Brandon was barely 11 and already noticeably overweight. We had pulled him out of sports a couple years earlier after we moved from Colorado to Cleveland. He showed little interest in continuing so we didn't push him. As a result, his food intake was higher than his activity rate and he put on pounds. Hoping to correct for the imbalance, we signed him back up for team sports — his peers were merciless. They called him "fat" and made fun of his size. Despite a nurturing home, his self-esteem was taking shots during his formative pre-teen years. It was clear we needed to try something different. In 2000 a friend suggested a local duathlon. She said there were no losers. People cheered for everyone, including the final finisher.

I made a deal with Brandon that all we had to do was finish. We could walk the run and even walk the bike. We walked. We were last. People cheered. We were both hooked. Over the next couple of years Brandon went from last place to first. He became fit. We moved from sprints to standards to half-iron, culminating with two

Escape from Alcatraz events. Brandon would place 4th in the 2005 USAT National Championships.

At a 2006 duathlon in Ohio, a poster was stuffed in the goody bag. When I opened it back at home, it was an advertisement for the Duathlon Long Distance World Championship in Zofingen, Switzerland. With Brandon's fitness in check, I quietly daydreamed about racing this event. It was just a dream, but I kept that poster hanging in my office for many years as a reminder. Every time I saw the poster I thought "what if?"

I was getting faster over time and in 2013 I managed to perform well enough to climb in the ranking systems. I received an invitation from USAT to attend the Duathlon National Championships in Arizona. I deleted the email believing I had zero chance of doing well in such a competitive field, let alone making Team USA. My wife talked me into retrieving the email and registering. I upgraded my equipment and secured a coach. I figured I had one shot and I might as well do the best I could.

The big day arrived. I was insecure and carried more body fat than most, but there was no turning back. I surprised myself by racing well enough to secure the last spot for Team USA. I was overjoyed! The following year I raced in the World's Long-Distance Championship and finished in the top 100 across all age groups. A dream fulfilled. A poster vision realized.

I gained confidence and each year I continued to try out for and secure a spot with Team USA. I raced championships around the world in all three duathlon distances — Sprint, Standard, and Long Distance. I experienced my first ever set-back a couple of years in, perhaps foreshadowing what would become my deepest challenge. After knee surgery in 2016, my physical therapists challenged me to recover strongly enough to make the 2016 teams. Pointing at their office "wall of fame" the lead therapist promised that if I make the Team, she will hang my jersey. Today my signed Team USA jersey hangs in the professional physical therapy offices across from the New York Stock Exchange. Right there between former patients and

Knicks players Carmelo Anthony and Andre Studomier. My confidence continued to build.

On April 7, 2018 I was limited to one national championship because of timing conflicts with a business trip. It was just the second year for draft-legal sprint racing, and I was stoked to participate. I trained well and was ready to make my 6th team in a row.

My readiness was confirmed when I had my yearly physical. Since I serve in healthcare, it was not just a quick exam but an "executive physical." An entire day of testing and poking and prodding and analysis. Reading the results, the lead physician exclaimed that I was in the top 1% of health for all men in my age group. More confidence. I never thought twice about my health given my medical results and healthy lifestyle.

The gun went off and I had a strong first run. I dropped into an excellent ride group and we rotated turns on the lead helping us all conserve energy. It was unusually cold and rainy in Greenville, South Carolina that day, but we managed not to slip. Into the second run I felt good checking my watch for stats and reciting all the things my coach had taught me. Focus. Enjoy. Breathe. I was ahead of one of my long-time teammates and friend Jeff. Using him as my barometer, I knew I was far enough ahead of other competitors. I just had to maintain my pace and I would make the team. Bragging rights secured.

At the turn around with about 2 miles left, my chest became very tight. Many thoughts went through my head. I concluded that my muscles were locked given how hard I held the handlebars on the slick road in the Peloton. One little slip and I would not only take down my fellow riders, but also our places on Team USA. My pace slowed and before I knew it Jeff passed me, encouraging me along the way. He encouraged me to draft behind him, but I did not have the energy. I thought about a heart attack but that was impossible! I had a super physical. I was fit and running fast. I was still running 7-minute miles.

I continued to reason with myself. If I am having a heart attack and stop, what will happen? How fast will I get care? I knew that "door to balloon time" was a critical measure in having a good post heart attack outcome. The longer the heart muscle is without blood, the more muscle that dies. Studies have shown that after one hour the heart begins to lose muscle. If you do survive, your heart function will never be the same.

So, if I stop, a volunteer will try to help but won't know what to do. They may panic. Ideally, they will contact a race official. The race official may panic and call medical. By the time medical gets to me all the way from the finish line, 30 minutes may be lost. There was significant traffic and physical barriers to cross to help someone on a racecourse of this magnitude. I concluded that stopping would only lead to what we called in the Army a "Cluster Fuck." Charlie Foxtrot.

I finally decided to outrun the damn thing. If it was a heart attack, I was likely within 10 minutes of the finish line. Medical was there. Perhaps it was my German genetic disposition, but I never quit anything. In a way, pride helped save my heart. I didn't want to have to tell people I did not make the team or that I quit. Hell no. I guess I was so vain that I would choose death over admitting I quit. Stupid I know. I kept running. Entering the finish there was someone ahead of me. I did an all-out sprint. I refused to be the defeated posing in anyone's finishing picture. They could be background in my finishing picture! I passed the person, grabbed my towel, medal and water and introduced myself to the Bon Secours medical volunteers.

It took a few minutes but thanks to mobile medical technology, the EKG was conclusive. Heart attack in progress. Images were immediately in the Cloud and shared with the team at Bon Secours St. Francis. The next thing I knew I was facing the ambulance ceiling, thinking about my family. And — did I make the team?

Thankfully the cardiac catheterization team was already assembled. They had an emergency case right before me and were prepared for another. Dr. Nesbitt approached me and explained the procedure. He said that he already shared the images with my colleagues at the Cleveland Clinic, the #1 heart specialists in the world. This made me feel confident heading into the procedure. I am an executive at the Cleveland Clinic, and these were all my friends engaged in helping me.

Nesbitt made sure I had a good view of the 60" screen. The catheter snaked from the top of my hand and into an artery. He climbed up my arm and into my chest cavity. Using dye, he used the contrast to find the precise location of the blockage. There was my heart — 30% of it was pumping blood as designed. The other 70%, limp. Dead. I had what is known as the widow maker. The deadliest of all heart attacks. Normally an instant kill. Clinically it is referred to as LAD. Blockage of the left anterior descending artery. In my case, a freak one-in-a-gazillion explosion.

Nesbitt placed the head of the catheter into the blockage and opened the valve. Like magic, the blockage dissipated in an instant. There was my heart. In full glory. Dancing. Pulsating. Joyful. Rejoicing! I wanted to get off the table and shout for joy — like David dancing naked and unashamed. Nesbitt wrapped up and asked if I had any questions. "Did I make the team?" He laughed and suggested that anyone who finishes a race with a LAD would likely make the team. And I did.

I was joined by my wife in the ICU. A nurse, she ensured I stayed within protocols. I felt super and completely healed but they said the first 48 hours are crucial to recovery. I played it safe. I was well enough to be discharged and headed back to Cleveland. The next day I met the world's foremost interventionalist who would oversee my recovery. Dr. Nissen, "I have the world championships in Odense, Denmark in 90 days. What do you think?" He smiled and laughed. "I know your type," he said. "Just be happy to be alive and happier if you can walk a few miles in 90 days." I played it cool but, in my heart, I thought "kiss off." I will recover fully and race for my country. I will do whatever it takes to be healed.

I followed the rigid recovery protocols. All my vitals were immediately available to my clinicians and my wife. All the technology I was responsible for at the Cleveland Clinic was now saving my life. I was allowed to run but had to maintain less than a 110 heart rate. My mile time was around 16 minutes. Basically, a fast walk. A few days into it I was able to get down to about 15 minutes and then 14 minutes. My doctor monitored my progress online. Nissen increased my heart rate limit to 120 so my mile time got down to 13 minutes and then 12 and then 11 and then 10. I could go any distance as long as my heart rate stayed under 120. With World's 30 days out, I was feeling good.

If my runs were solid, my bike was better. I could go above 200 watts of energy output without passing 120. The bike would pose no limits. I continued with a healthy diet avoiding alcohol and sugar. Dr. Nissen allowed me to go to 130 and my mile times continued to dive just under 8 minutes. Not world class by any means, but respectable.

Despite his experience, Nissen never saw a patient quit like me. He asked me to have a consult with one of his colleagues. Dr. Phelan's patients are primarily professional athletes from around the world. I met with Phelan who reviewed my chart and test results. He asked me one question. "Why do you race?" Wow, I did not expect that. I started to cry. It was surreal. It cut to my core. I shared that racing brings me joy. I was born to compete, and racing is a safe outlet. It helps me remain focused and gives me purpose towards being fit. It gives me discipline that I then use elsewhere in my life. It gives me hope. It shows me that with hard work dreams do come true. He put his hand on me and said, "Friend, you are cleared to race!"

Fifteen days before Worlds I was cleared to race! Joy! Thankfulness.

I just had to stay under 130. Fair deal.

We flew to Denmark and spent the first couple days acclimating and getting gear sorted out. World's always began with the Parade of Nations and team pictures. It was emotional. To think how close, I was to death 90 days prior and now I was at World's representing my flag. My country. My wife snuck into the Team USA parade line and held my hand. What a life moment. I recalled the feelings I experienced when I realized I was having a heart attack. That even if I lived, I would not be racing again. I felt so thankful.

At the start line I was nervous. I experienced a good amount of negative self-talk. What if I ran or biked too hard? What if I died? What was I doing here? Maybe I should just kick back and stop racing and play it safe? Was this effort worth it? I calmed myself by remembering that data was my friend. All I had to do was stay within my prescribed limits and I would be fine. I earned the right to race for my country and I would do it safely. I took confidence in all the prayer, preparation and medical analysis.

The gun went off and the field was already ahead of me. I didn't want any setbacks, so I stayed as prescribed at the 130 heart rate which let me move around a 7:30 pace where I stayed. The competitive blood inside of me was screaming but I kept repeating the adage that it is best to stay alive for the next race. It was hard to manage in the zone, but I did. Once I got on the bike, I could let the energy explode. I am not sure if it was nerves but even on the bike, I had to slow a bit as I was pushing 130. I reminded myself to enjoy the moment. To take in the scenery. To encourage my teammates and competitors. The final run was something else. I had to contain my energy and stay slow. It was humbling. As I turned the last corner towards the finish, coach screamed my name and handed me our flag. Old Glory. I bounded the last couple of hundred yards in pure joy. Tears mixed with sweat. Victory. I may not have stood on top of the podium that afternoon, but I accomplished something much greater. Life over death. Ultimate victory.

This story can't be told without acknowledging key individuals. The first responders in the national championship medical tent from Bon Secours St. Francis Hospital. The two paramedics who drove me safely from the event to the hospital. Dr. Nesbitt and team who performed the cardiac catheterization. The nurses and teams in the

ICU the first night. Dr. Nissen and his team who would take over my care in Cleveland. My own IT organization for the vision to integrate medical devices directly into my electronic medical record so clinicians could have real time access into my recovery. My peers who pitched in to ensure my work teams were well supported. Finally, my wife who helped nurse me back to health. Who created special meals and encouraged my recovery? My family, who showered me with love and support.

One year after my heart attack at the national championships, I was back again. April 7, 2019, Greenville, South Carolina. The exact same racecourse! Wow. Surreal. It was a little intimidating, but I was up for the rematch, determined to win. Again. I recognized the precise spot where I first experienced the LAD on the run course. I was looking for the spot. I am not one to use profanity or gestures but as I marked the spot, I gave thanks for life and then cursed it like a drunken sailor. I did a double fisted middle finger. I can only imagine what my fellow competitors thought about this athlete cursing the ground beneath him.

Before the race I made my way to the medical tent. As soon as I walked in, there were the same docs and nurses who saved me. They remembered me. One, it is not often they deal with a heart attack victim. Two, they recognized all my tattoos.

I tried to say something after "Hey do you remember me?" and I just started wailing. I was overcome with emotions. They came over and hugged me. I tried to speak but no words. Just tears of thanks. Tears of gratitude. I finally cleaned up and we took some pictures. I promised them I would not show up after the race. I did anyway but only to give them a thumbs up. I made the team! I shared with them my miracle recovery and showered them with praise and thanks.

Finding My Wings

Sybille Rex

Social support from family and friends is an important predictor of physical-activity behavior. It is difficult for an individual to maintain an exercise program if he or she does not have support at home. (ACE Group Fitness Instructor Handbook, pg. 97)

This is not a story about tragedy, illness or loss. It is a story of perseverance and re-defining the meaning of support which is crucial when we chase our dreams. Although we like to think of family as being supportive and right by our side when we need them the most, this is not what I always experienced. Not everyone will see our dreams as worth pursuing. It can be as subtle as a negative comment or a doubting question from people we respect and love that can make us change our mind from following a budding dream to giving it up right then and there, forever. That's what almost happened.

Triathlon started in the U.S. around the time when I was born in Germany. When growing up, I swam competitively during my elementary school years, picked up track and field in middle school, and rode my bicycle in every city and country I lived in. But it never occurred to me to combine these sports. And, I also never heard of triathlon as a sport back then.

My very first exposure to triathlon was in 2002. By then I was already living in the U.S. for a few years and I traveled to Germany to visit family and friends. By coincidence or perhaps destiny, I happened to watch a triathlon race near Frankfurt with a friend of mine. I was so excited by the action, the speed, the colorful race kits, the cheering crowds, and seeing the same athletes swim in a lake, bike and then run! This first triathlon memory was a fast-paced blur of color, energy, and joy. It left a big impression on me.

Fast forward to a decade later and my own short-course races. I tried the same reasoning to get my family and friends excited to come watch and cheer me on. Initially, when I was doing one race per year, it worked. But over time the responses changed. A few came to watch with excitement, some tried but did not love it. "We saw you only once." "We didn't know when you would cross the finish line." "It's not as fun as gymnastics." And others could not bring themselves to get up at 4 a.m. on a Sunday morning. These are valid points. I totally understand. In the very early stages of my triathlon journey, I relied more on family support. Over time, my desire to race became stronger than my fears of going to a race alone. I began to value that race time spent away from my family as precious "Me Time" where I would also get to meet like-minded athletes who became my other family away from home.

The year 2003 was life-changing on so many levels. Sadly, my parents living in Germany were headed for a difficult divorce. The ripple effects I can still feel today. But on the bright side, here I was completing my very first triathlon! It was a local sprint race near Boston, Massachusetts. Two close friends helped with logistics and watched the race. I trained for the race on a rented road bike, swam at the local YMCA, and ran around the park in front of my apartment building. Training back then meant being able to complete the race distance for each discipline at a comfortable, aerobic pace. It was a fun race where I finished mid-field in my age group. I was proud of myself!

At that time, I had no further plans to do another triathlon soon. My real adventures were revolving around mountains and caves. I explored caves with the Boston Grotto. But backpacking was my true passion: I loved to go solo, with friends, or as co-leader of group hikes with the Appalachian Mountain Club. That year, my biggest dream was to visit the highest mountains of them all — the Himalayas — by myself! I already practiced getting out of my comfort zone without realizing it. After traveling halfway around the world to Nepal, I fell in love with mountains that reached far beyond the clouds, and a welcoming, intriguing, and colorful culture. And my Nepalese trekking guide and I fell in love with each other. We got engaged two months later while looking at snow-covered mountains towering more than eight thousand meters high. There wasn't a diamond ring, but it was romantic and magical! Our Nepalese wedding ceremony took place in Kathmandu in May 2004. My husband arrived in the U.S. soon after. It was a whirlwind of excitement and life-changing events. However, I couldn't foresee the huge cultural adjustment my husband had to make. He came from a laid-back, rural, and community-oriented Nepalese way of life — to the goal-driven, individualistic, and super-busy way of life in America.

Over the next four years I raced two more sprint triathlons with friends, while my husband came to watch. But backpacking remained our higher priority. Then our life's focus changed when our first daughter was born in 2007, and it became even busier after our second daughter arrived in 2009. Those few triathlon races however, had left their mark.

The sport came into my radar again in 2013 when a new colleague at work mentioned the Boston Triathlon race. I remembered participating in this event several years earlier, and the fun I had. I wanted to try it again! The girls were older by then so finding time to train for this sprint triathlon was less difficult. I was hooked for real this time!

At the race I met more like-minded people and realized doing more than one race per season was quite the norm. I searched the internet, found another race, tackled all the logistics, raced, had fun, and met more people. Most importantly, I got inspired and learned new things — such as the National Ranking, an organization called USA Triathlon. There are people who do 10 races per year, now that's crazy! There are National Championships and even a Team USA! Wow! That was all over my head. I had a full-time job and a family to take care of. The National Ranking thing was a good place to start and check how I compare with other triathletes in my age group.

But that also meant doing another race that same season. I searched and found my third sprint race two weeks later, managed logistics, overcame weather issues and raced. A new triathlon friend said in admiration "Wow, you are so determined!" But my family saw it differently "You are obsessed!" That hurt! And of course, I wondered: Was I really obsessed? I expected praise, or at least some understanding — instead I was being judged. Soon after, I gave this no further thought because of all the fun I had, the incredible community I discovered, and because I realized that I LOVE the physical challenge of training and racing. I landed in the upper 50% of my age group that year and was thrilled. Despite my hiatus, I was doing well. And I saw room for growth, opportunities and new challenges. I started to dream big. Triathlon dreams: Age Group National Championships sometime in the future!

The new race season in 2014 started well, and not too long into it, something incredible happened. I received an email from USAT stating I had qualified for the Age Group National Championships — the Olympic distance — based on my recent sprint distance race. What? I was excited, surprised, and overwhelmed at the same time.

I DID qualify for Nationals!!! My dream had come true, and quite fast! But I had never raced the Olympic distance before, and there were only 8 weeks left until show time! The race was in Milwaukee, Wisconsin which required traveling, figuring out logistics, and racing in an unfamiliar location. I love traveling for vacation — but for an important race?

As I discussed these points with my family, they pushed back. Instead of getting help to resolve my confusion, they confronted me with questions like "Do you really have to go?" and "Isn't it enough to just race somewhere local?" I had no answers. To add to the difficulty, there are different cultural expectations regarding a mother's crucial role in raising children within the Nepalese society. Individualistic pursuits, especially for women, are not common in Eastern cultures as they are in the cultures of the Western world. Not going to the race would solve my confusion and make my family happy. That was the easy way out and seemed tempting. Maybe my husband was right? But, what about MY dream? Should I give up on it? What do I choose?

If it wouldn't have been for a neighbor and friend, who I told my predicament to, I would have never gone to Nationals. But she asked me the right questions. "How often does this race happen?" and "Will you qualify again?" The answers to these questions were easy, "Once a year" and "I have no idea!" But they helped me realize that this was a once-in-a lifetime chance. I needed to stand up for things that are important to me. Some decisions I needed to make on my own. I had to be strong! So, I declared to my family firmly, "I have decided to go to this race in Milwaukee this one time. I might not qualify ever again, but I want to see what it is like."

It was hard. I wanted family peace in order to train and race with a clear mind, without inflicting unnecessary stress on them. And ideally, I yearned for full support: getting cheered up when I was down and doubting myself and sharing the joy when I did well and realized my dreams. I wanted to be fully understood. My reality was different. It was a fine balance of finding compromise, clarifying communication, and being more compassionate. What really helped was explaining to my family what support I was looking for from them and why it was important to me. And likewise, I needed to ask questions to understand their side.

In August 2014, I went to Milwaukee and raced the Sprint distance in the Age Group National Championships. It was an incredible adventure and experience filled with learning, growing, meeting new triathlon friends and dreaming bigger! I was intimidated, but I also felt the excitement and special atmosphere that comes with racing at that level and being surrounded by an athletic field of that magnitude. And I saw athletes in the Team USA uniform with their name on their chest, and "USA" underneath it. That became my next big dream — far in the future, somewhere on cloud seventeen. I knew it would require a lot of hard work, focus and determination. And I had to get inspired and learn from the best. I made it my personal rule to always attend the awards ceremonies, get to know the top athletes, cheer them on and share their joy.

I met Richard at Nationals and we became good friends. His story and those of fellow triathletes have been helpful to put everything in perspective for me. I began to see what's possible, achievable, and what is "normal" for my family in terms of their experience. In the years that followed, he checked in with me, motivated me through setbacks and provided invaluable information. Richard also supported me at Nationals in 2016 when I first raced the Olympic and Sprint races back to back. He understood my goal of making it onto Team USA.

Every year since 2014, I qualified for Nationals and raced. It became my A race of the season. Racing against the best in my age group nation-wide was a challenge, and also one of the best ways to realize my next dream: qualifying for Team USA. The nagging comments at home eventually subsided and acceptance set in. I was determined enough to defend my decision to race Nationals each year.

The next couple years I raced a lot! Triathlons, run races, open water swims, and I had my sight on a Half Ironman race. I trained hard. I got better and faster, and then ... injured — a pain in my left foot. Plantar fasciitis! I didn't like that the doctor told me to stop running. I had to run! So I kept running until I couldn't anymore. I needed to postpone the Half Ironman race until the following year. However, I realized something else I love about this sport. I learned much about myself as a person, an athlete, my body, injuries and recovery as well as nutrition, training, mental strategies, gear and technology. And I keep on learning. This might have been my biggest motivator. Also, listening to my body is now a major part of my training, plus it has become one pillar of my coaching philosophy.

Despite my injury in 2016, I had a great race season. Another extraordinary thing happened next: I received an official USAT email congratulating me that I got a roll-down slot for Team USA 2017. I was filled with excitement, YES! Team USA! But I was also confused: a roll-down slot? What did that mean? Did I qualify for real? Once again, Richard came to the rescue, "What do you mean you JUST got a roll-down slot, girl? Other people only dream about making it that far! This is the highest level you can compete at! Congratulations!"

He was right! This was IT! WOW! It took time to sink in. My own mix of excitement and hesitation was mirrored by my family. In fact, I never received more excitement from them than what I put forward myself. I have come to terms with it, too. Lowering my expectations caused less disappointment and less tension. Getting any positive reaction was a win.

The ITU World Championship 2017 took place in Rotterdam, Netherlands, where I competed in the Draft-Legal Sprint distance. This was another new twist, draft-legal racing! It meant no aero-bars and drafting was allowed. It was yet another thing to learn and get better at. How awesome was that!

This event was extraordinary, special and challenging! Imagine traveling to a foreign country for a race with other athletes from all over the world. It was just like Richard had said, "the Olympic Games for age-group athletes!" The weather didn't cooperate until race day. But when racing at that level, one just accepts the circumstances and deals with them. I had to learn this here. The mental aspects of racing became much more dominant.

One of the best parts was the spirit of Team USA, along with the camaraderie, meeting incredible athletes and the support we received from Team USA management. Watching the top elite triathletes compete — LIVE — was the cherry on top! I took pictures with Katie Zaferes, Flora Duffy, Mario Mola, and Kristian Blummenfelt. I was over the moon and in tears! So much inspiration, kindness, and athletic talent! From then on, I wanted to be on Team USA for as long as possible. I made it my goal to qualify for the ITU World Championship every year.

Overall, 2017 was an incredibly successful year. I earned the All-American Honor for the first time, was selected to join Team Trisports, attended my first training camp in Arizona, and re-qualified for the 2018 ITU World Championship in Australia. That trip to Australia was another dream adventure filled with radiant sunshine, pristine beaches, exotic animals and plants, and an even stronger Team USA bond.

> ### *"A bird sitting on a tree is never afraid of the branch breaking, because her trust is not on the branch but on her wings. Always believe in yourself."*

Facebook Quote

The year of 2018 turned out to be another life changing year, athletically, but also career-wise. In the middle of the year, I left my stagnant corporate job behind and changed careers entirely. I had been toying with the idea of doing something totally different for a long time. Of all the ideas I had, I was never sure which one was right. I tried a few things, talked to many people, made plans, scratched some, failed at others and kept trying. The one consistent focus in my life — besides family and work — was triathlon. That year, I was selected as a USAT Ambassador and presented to various groups about the sport and my triathlon journey. A random conversation with a colleague about "What gets you excited?" and "On a daily basis, what do you think about the most?" led me to realize that triathlon was the answer for me! This was it!

It was hard to leave a stable, well-paying job behind, but once I made the decision, I felt a huge relief. At first, my family was supportive for me to take a break from my corporate career and have more time for the girls, training and racing. But over time questions of finances started to come up more frequently — and rightfully so. Those were tough questions, and I was in a pinch. Again, the easy way out would have been to find a similar job at another company. But my gut instinct told me otherwise. THIS was my chance to give it a shot, get out of my comfort zone and see where it would take me. The fitness industry and triathlon coaching were what I had in mind!

It was like a roller coaster ride. There were days filled with self-doubts and depression. Followed by days full of excitement and happiness when I felt free and fortunate to do what I love. Of course, more questions were raised by my family, and negative remarks doubted my talent. During those times, I reached out to friends and colleagues to find answers and guidance. They encouraged me to steadily move forward, without losing sight of my goals. I also learned that my own feelings of insecurity and doubt were only temporary and saying "Yes" to new opportunities could open exciting, new roads.

In 2019, I completely dove into the fitness industry. It was an exciting year overall, full of life and new experiences. Not only did I gain a lot of knowledge, I also obtained multiple certifications. My skills in instructing and coaching triathlon, swimming and indoor spinning were honed. Again, I remained on Team USA and competed in Switzerland which was incredible and humbling. I learned more about myself, while making sure our family was growing stronger together, and becoming more accepting of each other's differences. Support for our endeavors and dreams can come in many shapes and sizes and from different sources. I learned that I didn't always need to rely on my family to give me the support I wanted while chasing my dreams.

What I love most about my new career is that I have an immediate positive impact on other people's lives and fitness, and I can see that first-hand. It is amazing and so rewarding! Here we are, in 2020 — the year of the Olympic Games, a year full of triathlon plans, a year full of fitness adventures, a year as an Ambassador for the USA Triathlon Foundation and Nuun Hydration, and as a member of the nation-wide Team Zoot and the local Bay State Triathlon Team, and a full year of saying "Yes!"

It will be another year of staying open to opportunities, so I never have to ask myself with regret, "What if?"

What the Fire Ignited

Shay Eskew

My introduction to triathlons was no coincidence. It was divine intervention. I firmly believe God injects people in our lives at opportune times, and it's how we respond to those "coincidences" that determines the life we lead. Little did I know the impact of meeting one, Henry Forrest, would have on my life. I was a lifetime athlete who always thrived on competition, but it was Henry who **introduced me to a world with no limits...Anything is Possible!**

I'll never forget meeting Henry in November of 2007. I worked in a high-rise in downtown Atlanta and utilized my lunch break to enhance my physique. Or work on the "gun show" as I used to say. I would throw around heavy weights all to increase my chest and biceps, ensuring my manliness was intact. Well...that all came in question when Henry, then 64, approached me in the locker room. Little did I know he was a former Marine drill sergeant, one of the original 13 IRONMAN® finishers in 1978 and had completed an

IRONMAN® at 62. He said, "Hey, tough guy, why don't you join me and some ladies for my boot camp class." Intrigued, I thought to myself, did this old timer know who he was talking too? He obviously didn't know how much I benched or squatted, right?

I asked, "So what's involved in this little boot camp class?"

Henry responded, "It's pretty simple, basically all the exercises you did in grade school, pushups, sit-ups, squat thrusts, mountain climbers, nothing too crazy. Shouldn't be anything for a guy like you with all your muscles." Really, this 64-year-old had to throw that in there? I should have seen the bait but I never backed down from a challenge. So, I took Henry up and joined his boot camp class.

He didn't lie. It was all women and Henry, who obviously had no problem wearing spandex and a t-shirt as his standard instructor garb. For reference, Henry still sported a Marine haircut, was barrel chested, and didn't have the look of a typical 64-year-old man. Class started easy and progressively got worse. In 20 minutes, I was in tears and physically unable to complete some of the "core exercises." I suffered through another 20 minutes until it came time for pushups. I drew a sigh of relief and thought to myself, I'm going to show this old-timer who he's messing with. No sooner than we started, Henry dropped down beside me and started cranking out set after set of pushups. I couldn't keep up. He absolutely crushed me and there was nothing I could do. To add insult to injury, he then shouted in my face, "Ponytails is kicking your butt, you better pick it up boy." All I could muster in response was, "Yes sir."

I went home and told my wife the story and told her no one was going to embarrass me like that ever again. My ego was crushed by a man 30 years older than me. I made a commitment that night I'd work myself back into fighting shape. I started attending his classes three days a week for the next three months and was back in shape, worthy of a new wardrobe. However, during that period Henry was diagnosed with stage four pancreatic cancer and was given three months to live. Everyone was devastated but Henry didn't quit. He would do chemo in the evening and be there at 6 a.m. the next morning to yell at the class to get their feet moving. He made it a year, survived the "whipple procedure," and even built back up to long runs of 10 miles. Then the cancer struck again with a vengeance. He had only a few weeks to live. The cancer was incurable and had spread. How could a man that fit and that full of life have such a deadly disease?

Henry and I became good friends shortly after the initial diagnosis and we shared experiences after class that shaped our lives. Unlike Henry who faced a tragic diagnosis in his senior years, I shared my story of getting severely burned at the age of eight and enduring more than 35 surgeries over the past 38 years.

My story began on August 4, 1982, and like Henry's, it changed the trajectory of my life. My mom asked me to tell our neighbor about an aggressive yellow jackets' nest that swarmed my bicycle the previous day. I recruited my buddy Jeff (age 7), and we walked across the street and knocked on the door. The dad wasn't home, but the 15-year-old daughter was. As I told her about the nest she asked if Jeff and I would help her get rid of it. I preface this by saying I was raised by the most conservative parents you'd ever met. They took every precaution to remove all chances of danger from my life. I wasn't allowed to stay with babysitters. I couldn't do overnight parties. Or attend fireworks shows, jump on a trampoline, etc....

Innocently, and without knowledge of how to light a match, we agreed to "help" and stood 15 feet from the nest, watching as she threw a match on the ground. Nothing happened. We continued watching the yellow jackets fly in and out of the nest in the ground. Then without warning, a liquid splashed the right side of my face and shoulder. As soon as the match contacted the liquid, I knew what it was. GASOLINE!

Immediately, Jeff and I were covered in flames from head to toe. I threw myself to the ground. Luckily, I remembered to stop, drop and roll from the weekly "Code Red" tv show I watched, without fail. Seeing Jeff engulfed, I grabbed a water hose and extinguished Jeff's flames. I alternated the hose over the top of our heads hoping to stop the indescribable burning sensation radiating through my body. As I stared at Jeff and then at myself, I questioned "What just happened?" My body was charred and blackened. My clothes melted to my body. My skin was literally peeling off. When I touched my head all of my hair came out. Then and there I realized the life I knew — was to be no more.

It's hard to imagine three minutes of one day, in the life of an 8-year-old, impacting an entire lifetime. I learned very quickly life isn't fair and bad things happen to good people. I also learned we all have a choice in life. We can play the victim card and feel sorry for ourselves... or we can make the most of our situation and agree to never quit.

Never!

As a result of the injury, more than 65 percent of my body was covered in burns and burn-related scarring. Not long after being admitted, doctors informed me I'd never be competitive in sports again. My focus should be just on getting back in society. To make matters worse, my father's employer had dropped insurance on dependents. Our neighbor's homeowner's insurance denied liability — we had an estimated $2 million hospital bill. Fortunately, the Shriners Hospitals for Children heard about our situation and agreed to relocate my mother and me from Atlanta to their Burn Center in Cincinnati and treat me without charge. I spent the next three months at the Shriners Burn Center, 500 miles from my entire support network of friends, family and classmates.

Many don't realize what impact severe burns have on your body. My body was swollen beyond recognition. My unburned hand, the size of a baseball mitt. My head, the size of a basketball. I'll still never forget that first week when a nurse accidentally left a food tray in the room. Using my left arm, I was able to slide the tray forward just enough for the mirror to pop up. When it did, the image I saw in the mirror looked nothing like an 8-year-old boy. Swollen, contorted and misshapen. It looked like a monster out of a horror movie. I was so scared and devastated that I started screaming uncontrollably. The nurses rushed in and had to sedate me to calm me back down. That was the last time I looked at my face in the mirror for a month.

Getting burned was just the beginning of the 27-year journey from hospital bed to IRONMAN® finish line. I suffered multiple complications that materialized into severe infections, including the loss of several skin grafts (healthy skin that is harvested from one part of my body to repair the severely burned skin on my face, neck, shoulder and right arm) and eventually the amputation of my right ear due to gangrene. Initially, my right ear was burned very badly, but doctors felt they could save it before gangrene set in. Every few days the doctor would inspect my burns and especially my ear. I could smell the infection and was afraid to say anything for the fear he'd cut it off. The smell was intoxicating and I'm still hypersensitive to the smell of ear infections today. The doctor removed a pair of surgical scissors from his white coat and snipped off part of my ear until it started bleeding. All without saying a word. The bleed indicated the tissue was still healthy. After three weeks, it became clear the ear was unsavable and had to be removed.

By the time my last skin graft was completed, skin was harvested from my entire right leg (hip to ankle), left leg (hip to knee), a 4" x 8" section of my stomach, a 8" x 10" section from my back and a 3" x 6" section from my buttocks. When the surgeon removed skin from my buttocks, I asked that he not tell me where he put it, for fear I'd be self-conscious in public. Jokingly, I tell people now when my butt itches that I strangely scratch my face. Makes me wonder where the surgeon put the skin!

The most severe damage was to my right arm. The fire permanently melted my right arm to my side. My neck also suffered the same melting effect and was permanently stuck at a 60-degree angle. It took more than three years of extensive rehab, skin grafts and wearing three plastic, orthotic braces for 22 hours a day to correct it. Only then could I lift my right arm over my head and hold my head up straight. I missed the first two months of the school year, but my dad brought my weekly assignments to the hospital every Saturday. I even had to learn how to write left-handed in the hospital to finish the third grade.

To say adjusting to my new life was a challenge — is an understatement. In addition to dealing with my loss of abilities, I also experienced an overwhelming feeling that I just didn't belong. I was the only burned kid wherever we went: always. I also had to cope with kids at school calling me Freddy Kreuger from Wes Craven's movie, *Nightmare on Elm Street*. Accepting my scars wasn't easy and it didn't happen overnight. I spent months crying myself to sleep and praying for God to take away my pain. Eventually, I embraced that these scars would be with me for the rest of my life. And it was up to me to accept them and move on. As part of the acceptance, I vowed to reclaim my life as an athlete and redefine how people saw me. I didn't want them to look at me as the "burned kid." I wanted them to see me as an athlete. I truly believed if I could excel in sports it would give people a reason to look beyond my scars and see me for *ME*. And that's when my life took off.

My parents were advised to keep me out of school for six months until my wounds healed and to allow time for me to adjust to being back in society. Realizing life would never get any easier, I was back in school two weeks after getting home. My mom picked me up at lunch every day at school and took me home to give me a whirlpool bath and change my dressings. Two months after getting out of the hospital I started playing baseball. Fortunately, my dad signed up as the coach so he could make sure I played. He put me at second base since it was the closest position to first. I couldn't throw the ball overhand, but I could throw it sidearm. Six months later I played football. My dad inserted two additional inches of padding in my shoulder pads since I no longer had fatty tissue or nerves in my shoulder and right arm. I was by far the worst player on the team but for those two hours every weekend I truly felt like a *normal kid*. I never wanted a handout or special treatment. All I ever wanted in life was a chance. A chance to prove what I could do.

Three years later I was introduced to wrestling and it was a match made in heaven (no pun intended). I finally found a sport where it wasn't about who was the greatest athlete but rather who had the highest threshold of pain and could inflict the most amount of pain. Thanks to wrestling, I learned that hard work, the ability and desire to suffer, and sacrifice could trump natural ability. In the end, high school ended up being a magical period in my life. I was elected senior class president, established my identity and my confidence as an athlete. When I finished high school, we were 4-time team state champions. I was a 2-time state placer and set the school record for most pins. In April of 2019, I was inducted into the National Wrestling Hall of Fame under the Medal of Courage designation. In November of 2019, I was inducted into McEachern High School's Athletic Hall of Fame (my alma mater). Hard to imagine 38 years earlier doctors told me I'd never be competitive in sports again.

Back to 2008. Henry and I talked about "unfairness" in life and how our reaction to adversity determined the men we had become. We took comfort in each other's story knowing God had bigger plans for us and it wasn't up to us to judge how things appeared. We agreed we enjoyed so many blessings, how could we possibly complain? He recounted stories of his military career and how easily he could have been killed on the battlefield, like so many of his friends. I could have easily burned to death or lost my legs and arms. How fortunate was I only to be scarred on 65 percent of my body and still be able to run and compete? How blessed was I to find a beautiful woman to overlook all of my scars and give me five amazing kids? How fortunate was I to learn at an early age that anything worth having requires hard work and sacrifice?

Right before Henry passed, a group of seven of us fellow boot campers committed to Henry that we would race the next biggest triathlon in his honor, regardless of the distance. That race happened to be a half Ironman (1.2 mile swim, 56 mile bike and 13.1 mile run). We all spent the next four months training our butts off knowing Henry was watching, and we wouldn't let him down. It's amazing how enjoyable and invigorating the training became. It revealed a way of life where goal setting took on a whole new meaning. We learned the value of focusing on daily things and never losing sight of our goal. I never would've imagined doing one of those races had it not been for Henry.

Race day came and went. We sported "Team Henry" shirts and knew Henry would have been proud. The Gulf Coast Half Ironman was everything we hoped for. It treated us to big swells on the swim, windy biking conditions and oven-like heat on the run. I finished in 5 hours 38 minutes and loved it. I was hooked. Ever since I graduated from college, I knew a piece of my life was missing but I wasn't quite sure what it was. I was so busy being a husband and a dad, that I had inadvertently shut off the competitive nature of my spirit. I reclaimed my life as an athlete once again.

Surprisingly enough, a week after the race, our group of seven gathered to celebrate and tell Henry stories when someone tossed out the idea of doing IRONMAN® Florida. It was the same course but twice the length. I left the party and registered to race IRONMAN® Florida, five months later. Call it a miracle or an act of God, I raced IRONMAN® Florida on the one-year-anniversary of Henry's passing. It was completely unplanned, and I had not even considered the date until I ran into Henry's daughter the night before the race. I'll never forget her comment, "Daddy will be watching, and he'll be smiling." I knew then it was truly a God thing. Ten hours and 31 minutes later, I was an IRONMAN®.

Twelve years and three kids later (5 are under 13), I am still racing and doing things I never thought possible. I truly believe Henry was placed in my life for a reason and I'm so thankful my heart and my ego were open to his message. His words of wisdom have carried beyond triathlons and into my career. At the conclusion of the 2019 race season, I had completed more than 35 IRONMAN®/IRONMAN® 70.3 races, was a 4-time member of Team USA, ranked in the top 1% of IRONMAN® 70.3 worldwide for the past 5 years, and competed in 12 triathlon World Championships in

7 countries on 4 continents, including the IRONMAN® World Championships in Kona, Hawaii. I also competed in the 2019 IRONMAN® 70.3 World Championship in Nice, France.

Additionally, I'm a sponsored triathlete of Newton Running and an inaugural cohort of exceptional service-oriented athletes known as the Mālama Club, long standing members of the IRONMAN® Foundation Ambassador Team. To say triathlons have changed my life is an understatement. I can't imagine what life would look like without them. It's a lifestyle that enabled me to live my greatest version of ME. In 2018 I was convinced by my mentor Jack Daly to write my life story, *What the Fire Ignited: How's Life's Worst Helped Me Achieve My Best*. It is a legacy to my children on the trials and tribulations I've endured and how overcoming those obstacles allowed me to live an extraordinary life. I hope my message of "EMBRACE THE SUCK" empowers others to embrace life's obstacles as opportunities in disguise and to always commit to running — just one more mile.

Never Tell Me Never

Christie Petersen

Sports have always been a big part of my life, thanks to my active parents. Sports were how we played and had fun together. Sports were my happy place, my safe place. I played one year of NCAA Division I tennis before I realized I wasn't good enough to make a living at it. I changed my focus to get a degree in architecture. I now see what I didn't then. Nearly all the major accomplishments in my life were motivated by someone telling me I could never do them. Such as, going to college, playing D-I tennis, graduating with honors, obtaining a degree in architecture, finishing a half marathon, and getting a U.S. patent. Now, I love when people doubt me or tell me I can't do something. Then, I will fight with all my heart and soul to get it done.

The doubting started early, when I was in first grade. I fell behind in reading and spelling. My teacher said I wasn't ready to move on to second grade. God love my schoolteacher mom. Boy did she and my dad go to bat for me. Doing first grade twice was the first time I felt ashamed of who I was. I was given the learning disability label and spent time each day in the special needs class. Talk about the walk of shame! It broke my confidence. This was the beginning of sports becoming my safe place.

I felt like "me" when I played sports, and I never second-guessed myself. I was always the next team member picked in gym class, after the two fastest boys. I always made the honor roll, but I had to really work hard at it. I remember my mom telling me, "There is no such thing as a learning disability. It's a teaching disability. We all learn in different ways. You're smart. You learn in a different way than what most teachers teach." Tenacity, grit, fire, and drive. These were all the good things that came from my learning disability label.

Now, let me tell you about my greatest journey yet. It started when I decided to do my first triathlon. Peer pressure along with the fear I'd never lose the baby weight after my first child, motivated me to sign up. I joined a triathlon group and did my first group training ride on the road. I quickly learned that a mountain bike was no match for a road bike. I pedaled twice as fast and went twice as slow. I also joined the group at the high school pool for my first swim. How hard could it be to swim 500 meters? I discovered that running shape and swimming shape were totally different things. I could handle the bike and running, but swimming was my biggest hurdle.

After months of training, the big day arrived. Standing in line, waiting for my turn to jump into the pool on race morning was torture! Thanks to my anything-but-amazing swimming skills, I was in the back of the line. Many doubts ran through my head. "What if I panic in the pool? Why did I pay money to do this? What if I finish last?" At one point, the line passed by the restrooms, and I jumped at the opportunity to go one last time. As I was standing barefoot on the dirty, tiled bathroom floor, I had a brilliant thought! I could hide there until the race was over. That was until my sister's voice echoed off the bathroom tiles, "Hurry up!" I took my fears with me and found my place in the swift-moving line.

I crossed the finish line at the back of the pack. I was the happiest I had been in a long time. I accomplished something I once thought was impossible and had a blast doing it. Mentally and physically I felt young and excited again. I couldn't stop thinking about all the things I could do differently to be faster. My love of triathlons was born.

Seven years after my first triathlon, I found myself with two kids, working a full-time job, a member of Team USA, and a patient at Mayo Clinic. I was in the thick of my triathlon season when I hit two major medical hurdles. Like most dedicated triathletes, I dealt with the usual aches and pains. Then my headaches got worse when I worked out. The intense pain put me in the ER twice. My CT scan and other tests came back normal, so I decided to tough it out.

During the next three months I trained as much as I could, but the migraines, vomiting, neck pain, and trouble sleeping got worse. I also experienced vertigo. Despite my smorgasbord of medical symptoms, I still managed to win my age group and finish fourth overall, at regionals! Physically, I felt worse. With every turn of my head to breathe, the pool spun and the line at the bottom of the pool was impossible to follow.

I went to my family doctor. She was at a loss — we had tried everything. Jokingly, she said, "Maybe it's a brain tumor," and referred me to a neurologist. We both laughed at the improbability, and I left feeling excited to see an expert. It was July, and I had one month before nationals. I needed answers and fast!

The neurologist ran several tests, including an MRI. The next day he called and asked if I could come in to review my results. I thought, "That was fast! How nice!" The following day, I sat on the patient table trying not to rip the thin, annoying paper. My son was across the room, legs swinging from the chair, happily playing a game on my phone. Then, all I heard the doctor say was "bulging disk and brain tumor." I stared at my son as his eyes became blurry with tears. I thought, "No way! This kid needs and deserves a mom. Don't cry, you will scare him, stay strong. Brain tumor?"

The next thing the doctor told me was that my pain and headaches were probably coming from my bulging disk. He gave me a high five and left the room. I sat there wondering, "What the heck just happened? Am I going to die? Do I need brain surgery? Who will take care of my kids? What is a meninge? Or maybe he said phalange? Why did he give me a high five? Do I have to tell my husband I have a brain tumor on our wedding anniversary?"

The next specialist I saw was a brain surgeon. I learned I won the brain tumor lottery, hence the high five from my neurologist. If you must pick a type of brain tumor, apparently a meningioma is the one you want. Mine was benign, growing slowly in my right frontal lobe, and required keeping an eye on it, with a yearly MRI. There was nothing else to do unless it grew too big. Then I would need to decide on the option of brain surgery. It was always in the back of my mind. Or, in my case, the front of my mind. I got a steroid injection in my bulging disk and lots of physical therapy. I could sleep and train again.

I went to the USAT Nationals in Omaha a month later with a totally different outlook. The day before a big race I have usually felt nervous and run the race though my head a million times. That day was different, however. I jumped on my bike feeling calm, grateful to be there, and traveling with my husband. I wasn't worried about my time or how I would finish. As the road turned a gentle corner, the sun hit all the little glass flecks imbedded in the concrete. It sparkled like snow. The grass fields on either side of the road were a perfect green against the bright blue sky. I sat up on my handlebars and just soaked in the moment and thanked God. Just then a jet flew overhead and bounced to a landing a few hundred yards away. At that moment, I realized how small I was and how insignificant my problems were, compared to everything else going on in the world.

The next day, I had a good race and enjoyed every second of it. I thought I might actually have a shot at qualifying for Team USA, especially if I had a coach. Until then I was training with friends and using whatever free training plan I could find. I was so grateful to be back and felt I had been given a second chance. I felt blessed to be athletic, and it was time to put my gifts to the test.

That winter I hired a coach. I bought a Garmin watch and became a data junkie. I loved tracking my progress on Training Peaks. Knowing someone else was looking at my workouts made me work harder than ever before. I won a local Olympic distance triathlon and finished third in a sprint distance tri. It was going great and I felt confident.

Eight months later, I was on my usual Saturday morning, long run when my legs felt extra tired and heavy. No matter how hard I tried I couldn't go any faster. I figured I just needed a rest day. It was a different kind of feeling then in the past. I wondered if I was over training, so my coach and I dialed down workouts for a couple of weeks. When I saw no improvement, I went to my family doctor. After getting my blood test back, she sent me to a rheumatologist.

He diagnosed me with Raynaud's disease. It affects the blood vessels in the extremities and reduces blood flow. I can't drink a cold drink or grab a carton of milk off the shelf without my hands turning white. Losing feeling in my hands and feet was annoying but the pain from the loss of circulation was frustrating. If it's colder than 50 degrees outside I know I must wear gloves. I swim in our local pool with a full wetsuit and neoprene gloves.

Still suffering from body aches, six vials of blood, and a few weeks later, I was in his office again. I also had autoimmune diseases: Sjogren's Syndrome and Rheumatoid Arthritis. That explained my joint pain and body aches. Sjogren's affects the moisture producing glands and connective tissue. It can result in dry eyes, dry mouth, and issues with sweating. The doctor put me on Hydroxychloroquine and told me to buy some eye drops. I was very thankful I could sweat. I could deal with dry eyes and dry mouth, but an inability to sweat was problematic.

Like I had done in the past, I trained through it. I listened closely to my body. I was motivated me to work harder than ever. That August I qualified for the world championships in Australia. I couldn't have done it without the support of my coach, training buddies, and family. I accomplished a goal I never dreamed possible seven years ago.

I definitely earned it. I was physically fit, but I felt terrible. It was a sunny day with calm waters. My swim was typical, and I came out of the water 58 spots behind the leader. Cycling was my strength and I knew I had to pass at least 30 women to make the roll down for worlds. I ran into T2 after moving up 33 spots. I threw on my running shoes, visor, sunglasses, and bib. I headed down the road in the beating sun, no shade for miles. The last 5k to the finish line was all mental. I passed two more women on the way out and needed to catch one more. I saw my husband at mile five. He yelled, "Two USA kits in front of you. Go get em!" I pushed myself harder and left it all on the racecourse. With less than a quarter of a mile to go, my left arm felt numb. My heart was telling me to stop, but my brain could see the finish line and I went for it.

I took it easy during the winter months but saw no improvement in my health. My coach told me to focus on getting better and stopped writing workouts for me. I was worried I wouldn't be able to compete as a member of Team USA. I felt guilty not being able to play with my kids or cook my family dinner. My rheumatologist was convinced it was all caused by my autoimmune disease and this was going to be my new normal. No way was I going to accept that! I accomplished my biggest triathlon goal as a member of Team USA. Being on the team gave me something to fight for. I was not going to miss that race.

After multiple attempts telling my doctor that was not my new normal, I was at my wits end. I decided to bring my mom to my next appointment. She described how my symptoms affected my life and family too much. All the stress and frustration came pouring out of me as I sat on another patient table, sobbing my eyes out. My doctor realized how desperate I was, and he referred me to Mayo Clinic. Thank heavens! Three days later I packed my bags for Rochester, Minnesota. It was one of the most inspiring experiences of my life.

I met with a neurologist, endocrinologist, rheumatologist, and cardiologist. If they were an "ologist" I would have met them. Mayo Clinic was a special place. It was all about the patient and finding answers. They were some of the most talented people with many accolades, but you would never know it. The neurologist I met with told me to go back if I ever needed to have my brain tumor removed. Knowing I was considered a (forever) patient at the Mayo Clinic gave me great relief. He gave me a detailed explanation of my tumor, and it was more comforting than a high five. We planned to send him my yearly MRI, and he would keep an eye on me.

I also received much needed answers from the Mayo rheumatologist. After 46 tests and three visits I finally had a better understanding of my autoimmune deficiencies. They adjusted the dosages of my medications and took me off the anti-inflammatory drug completely. I bought myself an old-lady weekly pill dispenser, changed my diet, and added stretching and functional movement to my training. Every week I felt a slight improvement in my health.

I wasn't 100% when we took off for Australia, but I couldn't have been happier. I missed several months of critical training, but I was building up and feeling stronger.

If I hadn't been a triathlete and a member of Team USA, I would have humbly listened to my doctors, and accepted my symptoms as my new normal. The lessons I learned from competition and the desire to continue as part of the triathlon community, gave me the skills and motivation to meet my challenges. I have accomplished personal and professional goals thanks to my newfound grit, work ethic, and confidence. Being a triathlete is more than training and competitions. It's a lifestyle.

I hope my story motivates others to overcome their fears and personal challenges. Having a support system, discipline, hard work, and perseverance got me to where I am today. I believe all of us are all capable of more than we imagine. Triathlon provides the skills and confidence to be a champion on and off the course. It has changed the way I think, sleep, eat, drink and move. I look at food as fuel and make healthier choices. I respect my sleep time and go to bed early so my mind and body can recover. I drink less alcohol and move more. I truly think this sport saved my life. Instead of focusing on the negative side effects of my disease, I choose to focus on the positive effects of my sport.

I'm Still Coming Home

Jen Klouse

It was a normal day in high school, but the day seemed much longer than the rest because I wasn't feeling well. During the week, my appetite was low, and I had the feeling that something was wrong. I figured I would get better as the day progressed. After a few class periods passed, I went down to talk with my principal. She thought that it would be a good idea for me to be checked by a doctor even if there wasn't anything seriously wrong. I went to the doctor's office later that day. They took a few samples of blood for testing and didn't find anything awry. That night I came home after basketball practice, exhausted. I went straight to bed.

I made it through the following day, Friday, feeling much the same. It may have been slightly better because the weekend arrived, and we were all going to the football game that night. The game was against the neighboring city of Vassar. I was excited to see familiar friends. We won the game, which was a nice bonus to the evening. I stopped by a friend's house after the game to visit. I didn't stay long though, because I was beat, and my Saturday was going to be busy. My cousin TJ, and my friend Melody, were both getting married.

I was excited to go to TJ's wedding, because there were going to be some relatives present whom I had not seen in a long time. After his wedding, I went to Melody's reception for a while. I visited with friends there, and then I went back to TJ's reception. I had a lot of fun dancing with my family and just hanging out with everyone. I was getting tired though, so I decided to head home. I had a headache and wasn't feeling well.

During the night, I got sick. I figured it was the flu, because I had the basic symptoms of fever, aches, and vomiting. I didn't worry much and thought it would pass in a few days. Although, it got worse as the night progressed. I could not stop vomiting and started to turn yellow in color (jaundice). This got my parent's attention, and my mom sprang into action. My mom and dad immediately took me to the emergency room in Saginaw, Michigan. They rushed the emergency personnel along by telling them that I may have Wilson's Disease.

How did she make the leap to a rare disease so quickly? A few weeks prior, my older brother, Erik, attempted to give blood at the Red Cross. They had a consultation and told him they could not use his blood because of elevated liver enzymes. The doctor said it was possible that he could have Wilson's Disease. A rare genetic disease, that results in copper accumulating in the liver, brain, and other vital organs. I also had yellow rings in my eyes which was another indicator that I may have Wilson's Disease. We were both scheduled to be tested that week.

My mom read and heard about a doctor at the University of Michigan Hospital who specialized in Wilson's Disease. My symptoms worsened and the doctors in Saginaw decided to transport me by ambulance to the University of Michigan hospital. That seemed like the longest ride of my life. I remember specifically, the part of the ride, where the road was made of brick and cement. Riding on that same stretch of road today, still brings back memories of that ambulance ride.

I was admitted into the emergency room at the U-M Hospital to be observed. That meant more vitals were taken and more blood drawn. Then more waiting. Once the doctors checked me over, I was admitted directly into the Intensive Care Unit (ICU). I think I stayed in the ICU for about a week. The first two nights felt long. When people say they don't get much sleep in the hospital, they are correct. Every couple of hours, vitals are taken. And every morning at 6a.m., a doctor and team comes in to check how you are doing and feeling.

The first night, a few doctors came in to ask me a series of questions. They asked if I had pain and where, and they asked how my eyes felt, if I was having vision difficulties. The following night, the doctors told my parents and me that I needed a liver transplant. It was the scariest and longest night of my life. As soon as that was discovered, it was also apparent that my kidneys were shutting down as well as my entire body. At the same time, I was lost control of some bodily functions. I remember being in some pain but not much else.

Before I could be placed on the donor's list, I had to go through a series of tests. These tests ranged from having an eye exam and a dental exam, to bone density tests and blood tests. They checked to see if I was in proper shape to have a foreign organ placed into my body. My life was on a complete standby — at that point, my body shut down quickly, and I was placed as number one on the donor's list. In a matter of 24 hours, the doctors came into my room, and told my parents that they may have found a match. It only took 24 hours to find a match!!!! Unbelievable!! The only available information about the donor was that he was a 40-year-old man, who lived on the west side of the state. He was in excellent health and passed away due to a head injury.

The doctors began to prep me for surgery. The worst part was that pain medicine couldn't be administered before going into surgery.

I remember seeing my family and friends in the room with me. My mom told me later, that by the time I reached the operating room, I was in a coma. The doctors estimated I only had a few hours to live, because my body was shutting down so quickly. My mom also told me that while I was waiting to be taken into surgery, my brother Erik, and my mom and dad, were rubbing my feet and stomach. They also massaged my back to comfort me. I wish I could remember this, because if I would have died that night, my family would've been the last to see me smile.

The surgery took seven and a half hours. I woke up the next day to see my JV basketball coach, Coach McCall, smiling at me. I wasn't very responsive and had a difficult time talking with a breathing and feeding tube in my throat. Most of the time, I wasn't fully aware of what was happening to me. I remember asking the nurse a question, but it was hard for her to understand, so she had me write it down. I wanted to know how my brother was doing. He was one of the closest people to me, and to lose him would be devastating. The night before I went into surgery, Erik read a Bible verse to me: Joshua 1, verse 9; "I command you, be strong and courageous! Do not be afraid or discouraged. For the Lord your God is with you wherever you go." He told me to be brave and strong for him. He also told me that he prayed a verse for me that night: I Kings 17, verse 21; "And he stretched himself out over the child three times and cried out to the Lord, O Lord, my God, please let this child's life return to her."

While in the ICU, I had a liver biopsy to determine the health of my new liver following the transplant. After a week, I was reassigned to the transplant rehabilitation floor of the hospital. I remember so many special people who helped me every step of the way. But on that floor, I became closest with the nurses and assistants. I didn't understand everything that happened to me, and the nurses helped me to decipher my physical symptoms and feelings.

The diet I had for the first week was ice chips. All my vitamins and nutrients were fed to me through my IV. I didn't realize how important the small things are. It may have been only a small piece of ice, which means nothing to some people. Yet to me, it tasted wonderful — like a whole meal.

Each day, I became a bit stronger. I went through rehabilitation to get myself back to where I was before. That was very frustrating and difficult for me. I was driven to do more than I could physically handle. I couldn't walk well, and the doctors and nurses encouraged me to use a walker down the hallway.

It was very exciting news when the doctors let me eat regular food. I had a party in my head. I could have as much food as I wanted: pizza, ice cream, or anything else. I ate a lot of Jell-O. It was difficult to keep food down. My medication regimen was 40 pills a day. I experienced nasty side effects: nausea, aches, insomnia and vomiting. A dietician visited my room each day to give me shakes full of vitamins and minerals. It was part of regaining a healthy diet to support my weight and muscle mass, I lost 40 pounds.

Due to the kidney failure, I went through several sessions of dialysis, which lasted between three and four hours each. Some people say they can feel it. I never did, I just felt very sleepy. In addition, I also had physical therapy. Every day, I climbed a small set of stairs, one foot in front of the other, to make my legs stronger. The nurses helped me take a shower. I never thought a shower or being able to walk was so precious, until I could no longer do it by myself. I felt useless and agitated. I wanted to do things for myself without asking others to take care of me.

The most precious time in the rehab center was being surrounded by the people I love and feeling how much they cared for me. Slowly the fear of dying dissipated, and I was no longer worried about falling asleep and never waking up. The vision of my family and friends permanently stuck in my mind. I continuously reminded myself that if it was my time, I was going to a place much more amazing — a place with Jesus.

I received surprise visits from my friends at school. I was delighted to see them. I didn't care how or when I was going back home. I just wanted to find a way to finish my senior year and live life to the fullest. Surprisingly, later that same night, I was released from that floor. I was transferred to the Med-Inn, which is a hotel built inside the hospital. I stayed with my mom and dad and my brother Erik. The doctors thought this would be a more comfortable environment for me, with access to the hospital for various tests and blood draws in the TAC-U (Transplant Ambulatory Care Unit).

Erik and I became even closer during this time. I realized that when Erik gave blood at the Red Cross and was turned away — was the moment my life was saved. The week he was tested was the same week that I was supposed to get tested but fell ill. If we wouldn't have found out about Wilson's Disease from Erik's blood tests, I may not have made it to the hospital in time. It was amazing how God's plan fell into place.

Another surprise was brought to my attention when my friends came to visit. They told me I was on the homecoming court. I was so excited, yet I knew there was no chance I would be released in time to participate. My parents knew how badly I wanted to be there. Not just because I was on the court, but to also be with my friends, and be a normal 17-year-old again.

My brother knew how much it meant to me. So, he talked with my doctors to see if there was a possibility, I could be released the night of homecoming and go back the next day. On the day of homecoming, I was told that I could be released from the hospital, and it was such a blessing to me. Before I could go home though, I had to go through a session of dialysis. They also gave me two pints of blood to give me a boost of energy.

That was one of the most memorable moments of my life. I couldn't believe I was on my way home. My brother got a wheelchair for me so I could be wheeled onto the football field. The most special part of it was my dad wheeling me out and getting to be with my family and friends. I stood up for the first time in front of my other family, the village of Millington. I didn't care whether I won. I was just glad to be home. I wanted to have a chance to thank everyone for caring so much about me. I couldn't believe that they announced my name, as the queen. My good friend Andrea, crowned me, and the king was one of my best friends, Adam. I thought of many others more deserving of that than me. I was very honored, what a memory!

I missed my first semester of my senior year. My brother took off one semester of college to help me with my classes, so I could graduate on time, with the rest of my class. I have yearly check-ups at U-M and only take one anti-rejection medication, which I'll have to take the rest of my life.

I have been blessed with so much. Including, being a part of Team Illinois and competing as a recipient athlete at the U.S. Transplant Games, being a recipient athlete of Team USA, and competing in the World Transplant Games. I've also had the opportunity to be an international competitor for Australia's National Transplant Games, as well as for the British Transplant Games in the United Kingdom. The most precious part of the games is not the athletic competitions, but rather the relationships built with people from all over the world. Each person's story is unique and beautiful, while having gone through similar circumstances.

Taking Control of My Life

Kathy Kleinert

You don't have to be a certain size, weight, or have a perfect life to be a triathlete. You just need to be brave enough to believe in yourself and your potential. You must be strong enough to endure and push through whatever misfortunes come your way.

When I was 19 years old, one of my three older brothers tragically died in a car accident. He was in the Air Force, and at the age of 22, he had so much potential. I felt lost and devastated. I was angry at the driver that ran through the light and hit his vehicle. I regretted not spending more time with my brother, and I was sad that I never told him I loved him the last time I saw him. At that point in my life, I never experienced the death of someone close to me. Having to sort through emotions and confusion as a teenager was difficult for me — as well as for my entire family.

Later the same year, I had a lump that suddenly appeared on my neck and was growing fast. After a biopsy, it was determined — a benign mass on my thyroid. The mass and half of my thyroid was removed. The incision on my neck left a noticeable scar. The thyroid, which is shaped like a butterfly, is the powerhouse of the body. Thyroid hormones regulate vital bodily functions: body weight, breathing, heart rate, nervous system, muscle strength, menstrual cycle, and body temperature. It was a lot for a 19-year-old to take in, but I was very thankful it was benign. I was strong when I needed to be, and I needed to be at that time. I healed quickly, was able to manage the pain without much issue, and the other half of my thyroid functioned as normal. A daily low-dose thyroid medication was required to replace the hormones I no longer had.

At 21 years old, I married and helped raise two wonderful stepchildren for 11 years. During that time, I worked full-time and took classes at the local university. That left little time for exercise or anything else. I became tired, frustrated, and depressed, and I didn't know how to overcome it without prescription medication. I wanted children of my own, but with the current situation I was in, including a rocky marriage, it wasn't feasible. I turned to food, for comfort.

I turned 28 in 1998, the same year my dad was diagnosed with mesothelioma. It's an incurable cancer that affects the thin membrane, protecting several of the body's most important organs: the lungs, abdomen, and heart. He fought hard and participated in clinical trials and treatments. He had surgery to try to remove the cancer that was surrounding his lungs. His recovery was long and painful, and the cancer continued to spread.

That December, I received a phone call that my oldest brother had a sudden brain aneurysm and passed away. He was only 37 years old. It was completely unexpected and devastating. My parents went to their second son's funeral. My dad battled cancer for eight months and passed away only five weeks after my brother, at the age of 57. The entire situation was incomprehensible and seemed unfair. Our family was heartbroken. But I knew I had to keep pushing on.

Within three years, my weight ballooned to 260 pounds, and I was diagnosed with severe endometriosis. That resulted in a complete hysterectomy at the age of 32, negating my ability to ever have a child of my own.   After an amicable divorce, I spent more time and energy on helping my mom and doing fun mother-daughter things. It was hard though. She was depressed, had high blood pressure, and Type 2 Diabetes. She had friends who tried to keep her involved in things, but over time, she declined their invitations, and they eventually stopped asking.   My mom became even more depressed and didn't care about her health or much else. She lost two sons, and her husband. I didn't blame her for being in the frame of mind she was in. I tried setting an example and slowly lost 30 pounds. I changed my diet and focused on mindful eating, versus eating because I was stressed or sad. I was happy I was able to lose weight, but knew I had a long road ahead of me to be healthy.

There is not a magic pill for health and happiness. It takes hard work, dedication, and motivation, to change bad habits into good habits. It is easy to not care, and to eat for comfort, which is what my mom and I both did.

At the age of 34, I met the man who would become my husband, and he introduced me to running. One day I mentioned that my knees really hurt, and he suggested that I buy better running shoes — shoes made for my weight (I was still considered obese), foot position, and running style. I thought, there is no way a shoe could make a difference in my knee pain, but I was wrong. We went to a local running store, and I bought my first official pair of expensive running shoes. I still remember putting them on, thinking they felt like cloud slippers. Sure enough, my knee pain improved. My shoes made all the difference in the world!

Eight years after my dad had died, we noticed things were "off" with my mom. She was diagnosed with early-onset dementia.   Once again, my world turned upside down. I was losing my mom, and I couldn't do anything to stop it. My brother and I agreed to put her into an assisted living home. She needed more care than we could provide, and she could not stay alone.   Her dementia quickly progressed, and a few years later she was diagnosed with Alzheimer's.

Through it all, my partner proposed, and we set a date to be married. I went to a new doctor two months before our wedding. She felt the scar on my neck from the past thyroid surgery and noted there were nodules on the remaining half of my thyroid. After multiple biopsies, it was confirmed that I had papillary thyroid cancer at the age of 38. Within a month, I had surgery to remove the remaining thyroid, 30 lymph nodes, and three parathyroids. Recovery was slow and painful, but only a month after surgery, we married. My brother, my only remaining sibling, walked me down the aisle, and my mom was in the front row with her nurse assistant. It was my special day, and my mom was there — even if mentally, she didn't understand it.

Later that night, I brought my mom out on the dance floor, and she pointed at the scar on my neck and asked what it was. I told her it was just a scar, and I was okay. I never told her I had cancer even though there were hundreds of times, when I wish I could've had that talk with my mom. She would have been by my side every step of the way, if she wasn't going through her own horrible battles. Then she asked me if I had seen her daughter. I told her I was her daughter, and she said, "No, you aren't. Have you seen her?" It broke my heart into pieces, and I couldn't stop the tears from streaming down my face. Her memories were already fading, and there wasn't a single thing I could do about it. I held her even tighter in my arms, swaying to the music and feeling so blessed to be with her in that moment.

While postponing the thyroid cancer radiation treatments until after the wedding and honeymoon was a difficult decision — it was one I decided to make. I was required to be in isolation for several days. The thyroid medication was continuously adjusted, and I went in and out of hypothyroidism. It affected my weight, moods, and emotions, but over time it started to level out.

My mom was the kind of person that would walk barefoot in the grass and loved being outdoors. As she was in her final moments of life, I opened the window, and let the smell of freshly cut grass drift into the room. My brother and I were holding her hand when she took her last breath. Knowing she was no longer in pain or confusion, made it easier to say goodbye. There's not a day that goes by that I don't think about those I've lost. I learned how to be a stronger and better person and to appreciate the people I have in my life. Each day is a gift.

After my mom passed, I decided to take charge and be in control of SOMETHING in my life, amidst the chaos. I was obese and unhappy and often felt completely alone — even though I had a support system of family and friends who loved me. I knew that if I continued my unhealthy habits, I would most likely have the same issues my mom did, which terrified me. Something had to change, and it had to start with me.

With support from my husband and circle of friends, I went on the journey of losing weight, exercising and transforming, not just my body, but my aching heart and mind too. I found activities I enjoyed such as biking and swimming. I started jogging again. I had been dreaming of doing a 5K but wanted to prove to myself that I could do that distance on a treadmill, before signing up for my first official race. My husband surprised me later, with an engraved medal, "Kathy's first 5K – 38:16." It may not have been a fast time, but I did it. That was the beginning of my desire to experience 5Ks, 10Ks, half marathons, obstacle course races and more. I also tracked my food intake each day and started to drink more water. I had been obese for many years, and I wasn't sure what a healthy weight felt or looked like. As the weight started coming off, I felt increasingly better and had more energy. My clothes fit better, and I could breathe and move better. I lost over 100 pounds in a few years. I had good days, and not-so-good days, but I stuck with it. Was it easy? No. Was it worth it? Yes, it was.

In 2017, I participated in my first sprint triathlon at the age of 47. I will never forget how scared and nervous I was. I still didn't look or feel as fit as the other people around me. Could I finish it? Was I strong enough? Could I swim that far? Could I bike it? Could I run? Would people laugh because I looked awkward? Then I reminded myself that I wanted a fun experience, not a stressful one. It wasn't about competing with others — it was about doing something fun for ME. This was my choice, my challenge, and I was determined to do the best that I could do.

The swimming was exhilarating, minus the weeds and being kicked a few times. Later, I learned that was part of the experience. It was exciting to watch people speed past me with performance bikes and aerodynamic helmets. They were top-performing triathletes, and it helped push me a little harder. When it was time to transition from biking to running, I got off the bike and immediately wondered where my legs went. I started jogging down the trail and knew I would have to walk most of it. As I resorted to a fast walk, while gasping for breath, I felt disappointed. Another participant running past me said, "Way to go triathlete!" I looked around to see who he was talking to, because surely it wasn't me. I was surprised there was no one else. I realized he said that to me! ME, a triathlete! I AM a triathlete, no matter my size, weight, speed, age, scars or past.

As I crossed the finish line, I burst into tears. That finish line exemplified overcoming the pain and suffering throughout my lifetime. I proved to myself that I CAN be in control of something. That "something" is me. I thought about my family and how they would've been so proud of me. I thought about how proud of myself I was. My life challenges did not confine me, and my determination to push through brought me to that point.

Triathlons have changed my life and have given the me confidence and strength I never believed existed. I will always be running my own beautiful race, and I will do so with a grateful heart and a smile on my face. One thing I am certain of, beyond a shadow of a doubt, is that I AM a triathlete. I will never quit trying to be the best version of myself that I can be, even with the ups and downs of life. I am a healthier person, both mentally and physically. Of my three tattoos I designed, one is a butterfly with ribbons. Just like a caterpillar morphs into a butterfly, I too, can change and turn into something beautiful. I've had many days when I have doubted myself, but then I glance at my tattoos, and they remind me that I have overcome so much in my life too.

Fight!

Joe McCarthy

I was born on August 31, 1979, in Slidell, Louisiana. Shortly before I was born, my parents emigrated to the United States from England. My father worked in Aerospace and landed a job there. My mom turned 21 years old exactly three weeks after I was born. My mom was 21 with an infant son and lived in a foreign country. Talk about a tough woman. My father's job required us to move frequently, and my parents bought a fifth-wheel trailer, so I could have the same living environment. My parents were great at turning tough situations into adventures.

My brother was born when I was almost three and we settled in Baltimore, Maryland. In the third grade, my dad got a job offer in San Diego, CA. We packed up and drove across the country. We rented an apartment right on the beach and boy did I love it. I was always a strong swimmer. My parents bought me a wetsuit and boogie board from the swap meet and I was hooked. We only lived in the apartment for three months. It was a temporary fix while my parents found a home to buy. We relocated to Imperial Beach, California (IB) — the most southern beach in California. There, I got into swimming, water polo, and surfing. My best friend in high school was Ian Blake. Ian and his dad had a 1980's Volkswagen

Vanagon. On weekends, we'd take surf trips up and down the coast. They are some of the best memories of my childhood.

When I was in the eighth grade, my father took a job in Southeast Asia. My mom, brother and I stayed in IB. My parents were still married but my mom functioned as a single parent. She raised us tough. My brother and I were very independent at a young age. We were taught to respect people for who they are, always stand up for ourselves, and most importantly — get up every time we fall. She was preparing me for the road ahead.

I woke up early one Saturday morning to go surfing. I struggled to sleep the night before. May 11, 1996 was our high school league swimming championship. I didn't race because of my grades. I felt incredibly disappointed with myself, so I headed to the beach at sunrise for a solo surf session. Surfing was my therapy. The surf sucked. It was high tide, and the surf was small, so the waves had no power. It didn't matter. I just loved being in the ocean. After a couple of hours, I headed home. My childhood friend, Jacob, joined the Navy and his ship was coming in that day. My other friend, Tom, and I were picking him up. The three of us hadn't been together in about four years. Jacob moved to Washington with his family when his stepfather retired from the Navy. Tom, Jacob, and I grew up on the same street and it was great to be together again.

When we picked up Jacob from the dock, the first thing he wanted to do was surf. I had only been out of the water for about an hour, but I never said no to a "surf sesh". We headed to my house to pick up the boards, and we walked to the beach like we always did as kids. I had my long board, Tom was on my short board and Jacob was on a boogie board. During the walk, it felt as if we were never apart. We laughed together and at each other. It took the swim meet off my mind. It was just what I needed.

We paddled out 200 yards south of the pier. It was the annual Chili & Jazz Festival at the pier plaza, and we knew we'd run into more friends and have a great day. The tide began to change, and the conditions were different. It was shallow and the waves were steep but small. We weren't catching anything, so after 15 minutes we paddled north, right up against the pier. After I caught a few waves, I saw some high school friends at the pier. I decided to see what they were up to.

I caught a wave to ride in and was unaware of the sandbar ahead of me, because we paddled out south. As I went to lay down on my board, my skegs hit the sandbar, and I hit the bottom, headfirst. I was dazed. I lay there, face-down, for a moment and gathered my thoughts. I saw stars. I knew I had a concussion. Stabbing pain jolted through my body. I needed the lifeguard's attention. I tried to get up, but I couldn't. I broke my neck. I only had 15% of movement in my arms. I had to act fast or I would drown. I moved my arms the best I could to find my surfboard or leash. The waves made me feel like a ragdoll.

After what seemed like an eternity, I found my board. I used it along with a wave to turn myself onto my back. I was under water for about two minutes, and I felt like I swallowed two gallons of water. My thought was to swallow it rather than allow it to fill my lungs and incapacitate my breath. My next step — get help! I saw a kid playing on the shore. He was about seven years old. I called for him and asked him to get the lifeguard.

Moments later, the lifeguard was at my side. It was Oscar. I knew him. Oscar knew me as a local kid and knew I was a strong surfer and swimmer. When he got to me, I said, "Oscar I broke my neck." He called for backup and got to work. Within seconds, there were multiple lifeguards in the water along with San Diego Deputy Sheriffs. The deputies were fully dressed in the water making sure I stayed alive. I was back boarded and rushed to the ambulance. I remember feeling my hand flop on my chest, as they lifted me out of the water. The feeling was like touching a dead body. There was no time to waste. The next 48 hours were a blur. I was in and out of consciousness. I was right, I broke my neck and the C6-7 level vertebrae. Two vertebrae were crushed into 23 pieces. One piece pierced my spinal cord. In an instant, I became a quadriplegic.

I woke up Tuesday in the ICU. An incredible team of medical professionals performed surgery on me the day before, to remove the bone fragments, insert two new bones from a donor, and fuse my neck from C3 to T1. They held it all together with a titanium plate and four screws. I was in surgery for eight hours and it was executed perfectly.

I finally had a clear mind. I began a rapid-fire question session with my nurse. She filled me in on everything that happened. I was in shock. It felt like a nightmare that I couldn't wake from. All I could think was, "How am I going to get out of this?" I couldn't move or feel my body. I had tubes coming out of me from every place imaginable. I started to panic. Moments later, I heard, "What's up Joe?" It was Ian.

Two days before my accident, Ian and I got into a big argument at lunch, over a bag of potato chips. We swore we would fight it out after school. I told him we were no longer friends. It took a lot of guts for him to set aside my words and be there for me. Ian was there every day. He loaded up the Vanagon with friends and teammates. I was never alone, and that made a big impact on my recovery. To this day, I am so grateful for Ian's friendship.

Soon after, my coach, Mark Wraight came to see me. Mark was a father figure to me and the biggest male influence in my life at that point. Mark was a teacher, a long-time water polo player, and a swimming coach at our high school. Everyone looked up to him. I filled him in on everything. I told him I was scared. The first thing he said to me was "I don't care what it takes, I NEED you on the swim team next season." Mark had a way of motivating people unlike anyone I've ever met. He knew that was exactly what I needed to hear. I committed. It was time to get to work. I stopped focusing on what happened — and worked towards making the swim team. And I never looked back.

While I was in the hospital, I focused all my energy on moving my body. I tried to move my legs, flex my stomach, and wiggle my toes. Every time a nurse or doctor came into my room, I asked, "Did it move??" "No," was the answer. After three days, the lead physician came to visit. I asked him to watch my toes. They didn't move but my foot did. It was my hip that moved my leg! Within 48 hours I moved to inpatient rehabilitation at Sharp Memorial Hospital.

The hour of physical therapy and an hour of occupational therapy wasn't enough for me. I was used to at least four hours of intense training per day. After the first week in rehab, I began to exercise in my room. When my friends, mom, or brother would come to see me, they would help. They would grab my hand and I would do bicep curls against their resistance. I'd push against them to work my triceps. At night, I focused on trying to move my legs along with the other tasks I learned in therapy. The nights were hard, and that was how I occupied my mind.

The next day at therapy, I showed my physical therapist (PT) that I could perform the task and then we'd move on to the next. After about four weeks, physical therapy was more like a workout for me. We put five-pound ankle weights around my wrists and played volleyball with an inflatable beach ball. I lifted weights, rode the stationary hand cycle, and pushed my chair up and down the ramps. Visiting hours ended at 8p.m. Someone got kicked out of my room every single night. I was alone at night with only my thoughts. I was always excited for the morning and to begin therapy.

In occupational therapy (OT) I worked on things like cleaning my teeth, getting dressed, and cooking. OT was very frustrating for me. I was a 16-year-old re-learning how to brush my teeth after losing 70% of my hand function. My OT was amazing. She put up with my attitude and pushed me forward. After eight weeks of intense therapy, I went home, and my real work began.

I continued with outpatient therapy. In addition, I pushed my wheelchair to the beach every night and watched the sunset at the pier. The pier was my favorite place. Breaking my neck was the most traumatic thing that ever happened to me. I wanted to normalize — I wasn't going to let it take away the favorite pieces of my life — the pier and my friends. I watched the waves. I watched my friends surf. It was therapeutic for me. And pushing my chair two miles a day, dramatically improved my strength.

In January, I told my physical therapist that it was time for us to part ways. I wanted to move on and join my teammates on the swim team in February. My therapist and I had a heated discussion. The resolution: if I proved I could swim, then I didn't have to go back for physical therapy.

The following week, we met at the high school pool. My friends, mom, brother, coaches, and teacher were there to cheer me on. My teammates lifted me out of my wheelchair and into the water. It was my first time in the water since the accident. I held on to the wall as if my life depended on it. My physical therapist was in with me and everyone watched intently. My first goal was to swim a few yards, then swim 25 yards. My coach, Mark leaned down and said, "Fight!" That was our team cheer. It lit my fire. I let go of the wall. The pool deck erupted. I swam freestyle. My therapist was there in case I needed her. I made it halfway. I could hear everyone screaming, "Fight!" And fight I did. I made it to the other side in 2:52 seconds. One would have thought I won a gold medal at the Olympics! For the first time since my accident, I knew I would be okay.

Physical therapy was over but there was more work to be done. My teammates and I were at the pool every day working on my stroke. Within weeks, I swam 1,000 yards. I was still a natural in the water. Swim season started in February and my 50-yard free time was down to 1:06. That was a huge improvement. The training was hard, but I loved it. Coach put me in the 50 free at every home meet. I came in dead-last every time. I got a sympathy clap from spectators when I finished, but not from my team because they knew I hated it. I didn't need people feeling sorry for me. My best time that season was 53.6 which was about my 100-yard free time before the accident. I felt defeated.

When the swim season ended, the girls swim coach, Sue Czerweic began working with me every day. We tried anything we could think of to make me faster. It was exciting, fun, and frustrating at the same time. Sue knew me for years. I took martial arts classes with her sons. Sue was at the pier on May 11, and I begged the paramedics to let her come with me. They didn't allow it because they didn't know if I would make it until the hospital.

Steve Kal was my recreation therapist at Sharp. Steve was also a quadriplegic and the first person I met in a wheelchair, besides myself. Steve rolled into my room at rehab with a big smile on his face and said, "Hey, I'm Steve. I'm the rec therapist at Sharp. I'm here to help you get going. What do you do for fun?" All I thought was, "This guy is in a wheelchair!" I was so uncomfortable. I never interacted with someone in a wheelchair before. Steve turned into a great mentor to me. I told him I was a swimmer, water polo player, and surfer. Steve told me that swimming is a Paralympic sport, and instantly, I was intrigued.

In late spring of 1997, Steve called and told me there was a junior national swim meet happening in Mesa, Arizona that summer and I should go. I told my mom, and we immediately registered for the meet. I was classified to race with people in similar ability to me. We rented a 15-passenger van, loaded it up with friends and headed to Arizona! I won every event I entered. We realized something special was happening. I got home and went right back to the pool.

Steve called again the next year and told me about a triathlon and suggested we go together. The event was organized by the Challenged Athletes Foundation. CAF provides opportunities and support to people with physical challenges, so they can pursue active lifestyles through physical fitness and competitive athletics. I headed to La Jolla Cove on Sunday, and my life changed forever.

When I graduated from high school, I took an advanced swimming class at the community college I attended. For the first time, I felt like I hit a plateau. I needed to make a change. I was introduced to Alan Voisard. Alan was an incredible coach. He invited me to try his program. He also told me about Melanie Benn. Melanie contracted bacterial meningitis and lost both arms at the elbow and both legs at the knee around the same time I was injured. Mel was the first person I had a real friendship with who also endured a traumatic injury. We became very close. We were training with the same goal in mind — to complete the 1.2-mile race next year at the San Diego Triathlon Challenge. Mel and I trained hard that year and we loved every minute of it.

When I turned 20 years old, I competed at the USA Swimming Para Nationals. I held the American Record in the 50-meter freestyle and 100-meter freestyle, and S4 classification. Mel and I continued training together. Alison Terry was our teammate and an amazing swimmer. Alison trained for the 2000 Olympic Trials. Mel and I trained for the Paralympics.

The time arrived for the 1.2-mile race at the San Diego Triathlon Challenge. Alison was my guide swimmer. It was my first time back in the ocean since the accident. I was set to swim 1.2 miles, but I hadn't been in the water since the accident.. Go big or go home, right? A group of volunteers carried me down the stairs at The Cove and set me in the water. Alison was right next to me. Feeling the saltwater on my skin and the waves moving me through the water was overwhelming. For the first time since the accident, I broke down. Alison consoled me and gave me a quick pep talk. I strapped my goggles on and off we went. We hit the first buoy and I stopped to catch my breath and fixed my goggles. Al and I laughed, I felt wonderful. We hit the second buoy and didn't need to stop. We were headed to the finish line. I completed the swim in about 50 minutes. One thing came to mind, **I'M BACK!!**

The 2000 Paralympic Trials were the following June. I put all my focus into making the team. I dropped back to part time at college. I swam twice a day, five days a week, and lifted weights three times per week. I was a real athlete again. June came and the goal I set in the hospital four years prior became a reality. I was headed to

Sydney to compete in the 2000 Paralympic Games with one of my best friends, Melanie Benn.

I had an incredible 10-year career with Team USA. I competed in the 2004 Paralympics in Athens, Greece, and the 2008 Paralympics in Beijing, China. I was one of the first Paralympians to acquire a major financial sponsorship. I was also featured in a national commercial, as a Paralympian. It was my way to show the world that we carry the same value as our incredible teammates on the Olympic team. After all, para means equal. Paralympics = Equal Olympics. I retired after Beijing to focus on my professional career in the insurance industry. I wasn't completely ready to move on, but I knew it was time. I needed to focus on my future.

In 2017, my insurance career was in full swing. I was also 280 pounds. I wasn't focused on my physical or mental health. I worked with a company in San Diego, and I was miserable. I needed to make a big change. I found an opportunity in Phoenix, Arizona, and moved there in March 2018. I committed to myself to get back into shape. Shortly after, I began psychotherapy for the first time. I learned that I had depression. Throughout my life there were days I couldn't get out of bed and I ate to cope. I needed to cope with my injury, get my mind in a good place, and create a plan I could execute when things got tough. I hit the gym and focused on my diet. The following October, I was back at the San Diego Triathlon Challenge for my 19th consecutive year. I was catching up with Bob Babbitt, a founder of CAF, and he said to me, "You need to get a handcycle and start racing triathlon." So, I did. I was so fortunate to have men like Mark Wraight, Alan Viosard, and Bob Babbitt in my life. Those guys led by example.

Training and racing are now my anti-depressant. I'm addicted to the way it makes me feel. When I'm training well, I'm successful in all I do. I'm never looking back. I finally feel like I'm home.

"A man's character will not be determined by how tall he stands when he succeeds, but how quickly he rises each time he falls."

~ Joe McCarthy

Someday Tim, Someday

Tim Wilkinson

I remember traveling to the hospital with my dad, older brother, and younger sister. I can recall the exact words my dad said to us, "Your mother is going to Heaven." I wanted to run from the words, but I sat motionless. I was nine years old when my mom passed away on May 17, 1981. It was the day my life changed, forever.

I was an active child, but after my mom died, I became more focused on sports. In school I played a variety of sports — hockey, baseball, track & field, and lacrosse. But for some reason, I excelled at long-distance running. I ran my first 10-kilometer race when I was nine years old. It was the Terry Fox Run. I ran it in flat-soled, court shoes.

In October of the year my mom passed, my dad and I were sitting on the couch watching the IRONMAN® World Championships in Kona, Hawaii. I was in awe. As a nine-year-old, I had no idea what a triathlon really was, or the distances involved. I could barely find Hawaii on a map. I remember I said to my dad how cool it would be to run in Kona. It looked magical. My dad responded to me with, "Someday Tim, someday." That was the end of that conversation.

When I was fifteen years old, I competed in a triathlon. It was a relay, and as you may have guessed, I did the run. Yes, I loved to run. I did my first 50-mile-run when I was 17, the Al Howie Ultramarathon Classic. Most people progress to that distance — first run 10 kilometers, a couple half marathons, a few marathons, and then an ultramarathon. Not me — 10 kilometers, half marathon, marathon, and then 50 miles. I finished in 10:36:12, setting a record for the youngest in Canada to finish an ultramarathon. As a 21-year-old, I set a record for fastest 21 & under at 7:58. I've even run various distances on a treadmill, my longest was 50 miles (80.46K) for a charity, The Terry Fox Foundation.

Then one day in 2004, my dad became sick and was hospitalized. In one of our conversations, I said to my dad, "You have to fight, you have to carry on, you have to come and watch me race in Hawaii." He looked me in the eyes and said the same response he gave 23 years earlier, "Someday Tim, someday." He passed away on November 28, 2004.

I continued to run, and with more focus — Hawaii. I trained with more purpose than ever before. I drastically changed my eating habits and started putting in the hours. Countless hours swimming in the pool. Countless hours riding on my trainer and on the road. Countless hours running on the treadmill and outside. And many, many, many early mornings. I sacrificed outings, visits, along with the kids' gymnastics and volleyball events.

Next up, I raced in Ultraman Canada on July 26-28, 2019. The race took place over three days. Day 1: athletes swim 10 kilometers and bike 145 kilometers. Day 2: athletes' bike 275 kilometers. Day 3: athletes' run 84.4 kilometers. It was a combined distance of nearly 515 kilometers in three days. Each day we had a maximum of 12 hours to complete the distance. My number-one goal was to finish. I did, with a time of 31:00:06 (31 hours 6 seconds), 7th overall, which qualified me for the Ultraman World Championships in Kailua-Kona, Hawaii.

After 38 years, yes — 38 years — my dream came true. I was going to race in Hawaii!! After I stored that dream on the back shelf for many years, gathering dust, wondering if it would ever happen, it became real. I realized my dream. But how were we going to cover the financial expense? Paying for it was a different story. I had a deep discussion with my wife, Trish, "What are we going to do? Are we going to go through with it?" We decided to chase the dream and gather every available dollar, including coins. I have believed in many things and one of them has always been: coins found on the ground come from loved ones in heaven.

Indeed, many coins were found. Every time I picked one up, I would think of my mom and dad and say, "Thank you, I love you, watch over me, keep me safe." I would kiss my hand and point to heaven. The coins kept coming and my wife accompanied me on the trip to Hawaii. I raced in the Ultraman World Championships. While on the airport shuttle bus, I looked down and between my feet lay a shiny, new quarter.

Like the last Ultraman race, my goal was to finish. I did in 33:29:10, 19th overall. One sentence I always wanted to say was, "I punched my ticket to race on the World Stage." I was finally able to say it. When I was asked, "Would you race the race again?" Immediately I replied, "Absolutely, in a heartbeat!!"

I never gave up on my dream, not once did it cross my mind to quit. Not once.

Don't give up on a dream because of the length of time it will take. Time will pass anyway. I'm proof of that. Chase your dreams as I did. Die First. Then quit.

After the race in Hawaii, my wife and I went for a long walk on the beach at a nearby resort. While walking on the beach path, I thanked her for helping me realize my dream of racing in Hawaii. Along one edge of the beach, the lava rock was black. People placed white rocks on the lava rock to spell out words and names. As we walked along, Trish stopped abruptly and gasped, "Look at that." She pointed to a gathering of white rocks that were in the shape of a heart with the name "Al" in the middle of it. We stood motionless. That time I did not want to run. I took a deep breath and whispered, "Someday Tim, someday."

"Al" was my dad's name. Holy crap!!

Photo from www.bob-haller.eu

Ever Forward

Bob Haller

Hello, I am Bob Haller, and to clarify something right away, I am not related to Valerie Haller or her husband Thomas in any direct way. I am a professional triathlete from Luxembourg. I have been competing in triathlons since 2007, and I have raced in over 100 triathlon competitions. My current International Triathlon Union (ITU) world ranking is 70 and my goals for the year are to rank among the top 50 in the world and compete in the Olympic Games in Tokyo.

Like many triathletes, I too have a story. I have mixed feelings about a race from 2015. The joys and disappointment of that race still clash within me today. It was the first ever European Games held at Bilgah Beach in Baku, Azerbaijan. I qualified for the games as the first and only triathlete from Luxembourg. A great honor to represent my country along with 57 of the best triathletes from around the world. The winner would earn a spot to compete in the Olympics in Rio.

The day began with scorching temperatures and for some reason, which I cannot fully explain today, I wore a black tri-suit. We lined up on Bilgah Beach according to our ranking. I was number 24 (European ranking) and I felt the adrenaline begin to build. Seconds later, the race horn sounded and into the water I went. The race was on. I kept pace with the top swimmers, pulling hard through the water and not giving in to the fatigue I began to feel. I came out of the water less than a minute behind the leader. I pushed myself as I ran. Every second counts in the shorter distance triathlons, and I wanted to gain a few seconds on my way into the transition area.

Up next was the bike. My transition onto the bike was smooth, and I found myself in a large chase pack with the leaders in sight. On the third lap, the gap closed. I was in the front portion of the pack as we overtook the lead group. As we jockeyed for positions, tension among the cyclists rose. We watched each other closely and anticipated a move. Sure enough, one came a few minutes later. Bishop, from Britain, darted out while two others sat up briefly, slowed the rest of the group and gave Bishop a slight gap. When I saw the move and felt the pack slow slightly, a second Britain, Benson, broke away. Without hesitation, I grabbed his wheel and followed him out of the pack. A few others joined me and Benson, and we caught up to Bishop.

It was time to work together and put some distance between our lead of nine and the chase pack. I felt the adrenaline rush again as I took a turn at the front, pulling the pack. I wanted to keep the pace high, with hope that would burn a few of the legs on the others in the group. I peeled off the front to settle in and fuel-up for the run. I reached for the gel packet, slurped down the remains and tossed the packet aside. Each time I got to the front, I pushed hard. I had the third-best bike time of the day, only three seconds from first.

The nine of us finished the bike course as a group but with a nice gap ahead of the pack.

Another smooth transition off the bike. I ran in fifth place, just off the shoulders of the lead runners. A possible podium position was within reach. "Stay calm and focused. You trained for this," were the thoughts running through my head. My race was going as planned when suddenly disappointment hit. A penalty marker flashed at me. Yes — a penalty. Earlier in the race when I discarded my gel packet, I did so outside of the littering zone, and the entire world saw it — live. A penalty would take away the precious seconds I so desperately worked to gain. I served my penalty as I watched several athletes run by. It broke me. I was disappointed in myself. I knew better. I let the excitement of the race and the adrenaline rush, momentarily cloud my judgement. In a split second, the podium position vanished.

I finished the race in 20th position, and to my surprise, I was met at the finish line by Luxembourg's Grand Duke Henri. Tears welled up in my eyes as we talked. I was honored to meet Duke Henri and hear his kind words of support and encouragement. I was also sad that in a fleeting moment, I made an error and lost the possibility of a podium position for my country.

Since then, I've spent time thinking about my performance and the results of that race. I walked away with a few lessons that many athletes may find helpful. First, we are not defined solely by any one event. The result of one race, one exam, one decision does not fully represent who and what we are. We are an accumulation of all our mistakes, all our triumphs, and all our experiences. When disappointment comes or tragedy strikes — focus on yourself as a whole individual and stay mindful of all that you are.

Second, as triathletes, we run into problems during races. They could be mechanical problems, crashes, rule violations, stumbles in transition, difficult swims, or just "off" days. We might even have a tragedy that strikes us in our daily lives. Whatever it might be, we must not let these events affect us beyond the current moment. We can't stay upset or angry with what has happened. We must keep moving forward to the next moment. A former coach who passed away a few years ago would frequently say, "Ever forward!" During a race, we collect ourselves and continue racing. In life, we can pull ourselves up, turn the page and write new chapters. I have taken my coach's words to heart and use them as inspiration. I invite you to do the same...

EVER FORWARD!

Triathlon Trials and Tribulations

Tenchi So

"There's an old saying in Tennessee — I know it's in Texas, probably in Tennessee — that says, fool me once, shame on — shame on you. Fool me [twice] — you can't get fooled again."

~ George W. Bush, 43rd President of the United States

Many people join the great sport of triathlon for various reasons. Whether they look for a new challenge, go outside their comfort zones, overcome a tragedy or hardship, or fight against illness — they embrace the good and bad that inevitably comes with the journey. My nearly six-year triathlon journey has certainly been an interesting ride through the valley of self-discovery, and a dogfight to prove to myself, that I can rise to the challenges.

I am a former Infantry Officer with the Canadian Forces and a lifelong martial artist who switched to triathlons in May 2014. Since then, I have raced 29 x 70.3s (Half-Ironman) and 9 x 140.6s (IRONMAN®) around the world, mostly with the IRONMAN® branded races run by the World Triathlon Corporation (WTC). I got into triathlons because I enjoy competing and love to travel. Every time I raced — I went on "Race-cations" which was quite wonderful.

Since I started triathlons, I have raced all over the United States, Canada, Brazil, Spain, Denmark, Germany, and Mexico.

Before I switched to triathlons, I dabbled in cross-country and indoor track in high school and university. My athletic career was spent doing martial arts in many forms: karate, boxing, Tae Kwon Do, Hapkido, and as a competitive Muay Thai fighter in my late twenties. My last sport was K-1 kickboxing. I had no background in swimming and was hesitant about that part of triathlons. It really scared me, but I decided to pull the trigger and learn how to swim.

My first swim coach, Lorene, was wonderful. She was a former 8-time Canadian Paralympic triathlon champion who knew how to teach. She taught me all the fundamentals of swimming, as well as specific techniques that helped me be more efficient in the water. Due to my previous head injuries incurred in my military and martial arts career, I simply could not do flip turns in the pool. She even took the time to teach me an alternative to flip turns — open wall turns. She made swimming fun, and I started to look forward to it. Unfortunately, after a few months I had to discontinue my swim training with Lorene due to distance and looked for another master's triathlon swim club closer to where I lived.

That was where the perfect storm of bad luck began, and my newfound love of swimming disappeared. My second swim coach, a former ITU Pro Triathlete, made swimming unpleasant and hampered my growth.

I remember she yelled at me and called me by another person's name in front of everyone. She thought that I was another Asian swimmer. When I corrected her, she defended her mistake by saying, "You Asians all look alike." It was not only unprofessional but reeked of bigotry and a monocultural view of the world. I was shocked by what I heard.

Another clear display of poor leadership came in a form of "bribing" us with $20 prior to our swim time trial. The deal was that one could keep the $20 if one beat the prior 400m PB time but give it back if the time wasn't beat. She probably thought that was a great way to motivate the team, but I found it more insulting than anything. One may ask why I didn't leave the swim team or report her. I must admit I'm a stubborn individual. I stuck around for another two years to make sure she got her comeuppance. I knew I frustrated her every time I showed up on the pool deck, and I enjoyed every minute of it.

There came a time when I was willing to call a truce. However, she didn't have the maturity and courage to talk to me in person, and she made every excuse to avoid me. My rationale in hiring her was she's a former IRONMAN® pro, she's going to help me be a good long-course distance racer. Right? Well, fuck me, in the three and a half years that I worked with that coach, I essentially did not improve. She did not properly prescribe the right workouts to stimulate my physiology and improve my endurance to succeed in long-course racing.

I was baffled that she never heard of the 80/20 training principle — where 80% is done easy and 20% is done hard. Given my background as a martial artist, what I needed to work on was on my aerobic fitness, in order to have the endurance to keep a fast pace throughout the race. Every workout she prescribed was done at high intervals or high aerobic threshold — day in, day out. What happened to Maximum Aerobic Function (MAF) and polarized training??? W.T.F. Who focuses on nothing but high-aerobic speed workouts to build endurance? How can anyone with virtually no aerobic fitness or endurance compete at long-course racing without an endurance base?

I burned out daily. It was a miracle that I wasn't injured during the years I worked with Coach "Numbnuts." I can only speculate that my experience in the military and martial arts made me somewhat resilient to the high stress. My body was already used to training hard and operating in high-stress environments.

To build endurance and aerobic fitness, a triathlete must swim, bike, and run EASILY! A triathlete must swim, bike, and run below the athlete's personal aerobic threshold! That was a good reminder to always listen to my gut instinct and do my own research.

The recent tests at the University of Denver's Sports Medicine and Performance Centre confirmed my suspicions. For the first two seasons, I followed the 80/20 training principle, but my progress stalled after I hired and started with Coach "Numbnuts". Coincidence? I think not.

The findings and recommendations were quite simple...focus on 80/20 training. I had to ensure that I did 80% of my training easily in sub-threshold, and 20% of my training in threshold and above.

Indeed, gaining and developing endurance through high-end intervals was possible, but for me, that approach was the same as trying to salvage the last couple pieces of orange pulp from an empty orange juice carton — it was more effort than it was worth. It would have been much better to get a new carton — and instead train my aerobic base through zone one and two training. My high aerobic capacity was simply maxed out and trying to build more aerobic base through high-end intervals did not yield improvements.

My luck is about to change with my current coach, a former pro triathlete from the pioneering days of the 80's. He has been heavily involved in the triathlon community since. He understood my issues and background when I spoke with him. I started working with him in August 2019 and he was able to help turn things around for me, despite my busy life and race schedule.

I do believe that the culture of triathlon needs to change with respect to holding coaches accountable. There are too many instances when an athlete is blamed for a bad performance, but the coaches are not questioned and are given the benefit of the doubt. The attitude of blaming an athlete is insane, given other professional sport teams, such as NHL, NFL, MBA, CFL, etc. They fire their head coaches if the team does not perform well. I would love to see more coaches held accountable for their athlete's performances. Consider what happened to Paula Findlay, when she finished dead last at the 2012 London Olympics. Her coaches blamed her and tried to skirt out of blame, which was shameful.

I have the challenge of racing unconventionally. Unlike most of the age groupers, I don't tactically choose my races (or cherry pick them). I base my race selection on where I want to travel. In doing so, I am at the mercy of the destination's weather, which has never been favorable for me, yet. Racing in different countries year-round and in different environments sounds exotic and exciting. But the race conditions play a huge factor in performance, along with travel fatigue, jet lag, and how the body copes with a new environment.

I have been quite unlucky, particularly in IRONMAN® races. That may come off as an excuse, but in all my IRONMAN® races, locals and commentators have confirmed that the weather was the worst they've had for a race. IRONMAN® Cozumel, which I raced in November 2019 was a perfect example — many have dubbed the 2019 edition of the race as the "Mexican-Kona".

But I will own that mistake proudly. Even though it may not be a standard practice to do so, I still raced without the proper aerobic training. It showed the power of the human mind, and that it is possible to achieve something once thought of as impossible. After all, who races close to 30 - 70.3 races and nine 140.6s in five years?

I'm back to 80/20 training and hoping for more positive results in the 2020 season. It's going to take time to properly acquire and improve my aerobic fitness, but with my new coach's guidance, I am beginning to see results.

Remember to believe and trust in yourself. Believe in the process and enjoy the trek that will propel your journey of self-discovery.

You know yourself better than anyone. So, don't be afraid to do your own research — ask lots of questions, think outside of the box, and don't be afraid to do something different.

I am confident that I have been able to resolve my own issues coming into this sport and can now focus on being competitive. I intend to qualify for both IRONMAN® 70.3 and IRONMAN® World Championships soon, as well as the competitive age group category in which I belong.

As the former professional and 2012 IRONMAN® World Champion, Pete Jacobs, wrote on his Twitter account, the day of the fateful 2019 IRONMAN® World Championships, when reigning champion Jan Frodeno won and broke the new record: "To everyone racing [#IMWC] tomorrow, be strong, present, grateful & confident, & then all the other important stuff will look after itself. You'll be calmer, smarter, more efficient, & faster. Good luck. #yougotthis.

It's What You Do That Defines You

Scott Baranek

On numerous occasions, people have told me that I inspire them. I used to hate it. To me, it meant they noticed I was different. My reasons for doing the things that I have done, were not for inspiration. They were to adapt for the things I did before, when I lived a "normal" life. As I've grown older, I've changed my position on being inspirational.

If you need a reason to believe — in your own strength to accomplish something — then let me be your example.

My story began on a Friday evening, September 2, 1994. I was 23 years old when my life changed forever. On the way home from work, my motorcycle was hit by a car turning left, from the oncoming lane. I landed in a ditch 138 feet from the point of impact. My left leg was twisted underneath me. As I struggled to pick my leg up, my foot dangled from my body, connected only by the calf muscle. I lay there bleeding profusely. I knew that in order to survive, I would lose my left leg.

Prior to the accident, I lived an active lifestyle. I have always been passionate about sports. I played several sports through middle school and high school — and I dominated. I joined the Navy after high school where I learned about mental and physical strength. When I returned, I spent countless hours working out or playing basketball. Before the summer of 1994, I developed a passion for waterskiing.

When I lay in that ditch, I could not imagine how I could live my life without my leg. Before my accident, I used to say, "In life there are participants and there are spectators." I was not mentally prepared to live as a spectator.

My foot was amputated just below the knee, five days after the accident. "Boy, were you lucky," they told me. I laughed when I heard that. I responded, "If I was lucky, the car would have missed." I focused on being alive and appreciating life. I focused on what I had: three good limbs, my left knee, no head injury, and no paralysis. I strived to understand it could have been worse. People said, "You're so positive, I could never cope with that." My response was, "You don't know what you'll do until you're in that situation." The truth was, I never would have chosen the path I am on now. And today — I would never want to be anyone else.

I rose to the challenge of physical activities that seemed intimidating to some people. Back in the day, I was 6' 5", and weighed 224 pounds. A desire to compete and challenge still burned inside of me after my leg was amputated. I decided to return to my passion of waterskiing to provide the thrill-seeking and physical-activity I wanted from life. That was the first of many challenges I faced adapting to the world as an amputee.

I reconnected with the close circle of friends I skied with prior to the accident. I was bobbing in the water behind Tod's Mastercraft ski boat, when doubts filled my mind. "Can I really do this? What if I fail? Have I been fooling myself this whole time? What if I can't do this?" I was afraid of failure. I told everyone I was going to do it, and the moment of truth had arrived. I was a slalom skier, one ski. But I still needed two legs. My left leg and prosthetic foot would be in the back working as the rudder. I did not have sensation in my left foot. And I didn't have an ankle or toes to slide into the boot. I took a deep breath and gave the go sign — the challenge was on. I got up, out of the water. That was the first goal.

It was unsatisfactory to me, but impressive to others who saw me as an amputee. To me, skiing did not mean only getting up and out of the water. I needed ski as good as anyone else. My feeling of accomplishment was short lived. I did not get the feedback from my foot, so I learned to use my hips. I learned to focus on what I do have and how to make that work. In my moments of frustration, I was focused on what I didn't have, my foot. Once I shifted the focus to adapting with what I had, it was like a light appeared to show me the way.

I learned two important lessons that summer — I can adapt by persevering, and to remove the limitations I put on myself as an amputee. Since then, I have lived my life moving beyond my comfort zone and set my mind to challenge myself and accomplish new goals. I have gone on to do whatever I want. In addition, I am a prosthetist who provides educational resources and training for those with prosthetic limbs.

While running and wearing my prosthetic limb, I am often asked, "How much of an advantage do you have running with a prosthetic foot?" There is no advantage, only a disadvantage. There was a bi-lateral amputee, who wanted to run in the Olympics. The Olympic committee ruled against him because the prosthetic limbs (the blades) gave him an unfair competitive advantage. That ruling was a disservice to the amputee community. Amputees are less than one percent of the population, so there is not much understanding of the challenges of living with a prosthetic limb. The reality is — anyone living an active lifestyle with a prosthetic limb is enduring a certain amount of pain to do so.

On August 8, 2009 I competed in my first triathlon, The Sanford and Sun in Sanford, Michigan. A good friend, Dr. Michael Sullivan, presented the idea and it sounded good, except for the run. I swam a little to train and put road tires on an old mountain bike. I didn't have a good training plan in place, but then again, I didn't know what I was doing. I completed several 500-meter swims and twice as many 20k bike rides. The running did not go so well. When I finished a 5k run, I needed at least five days to heal before another run. And I couldn't complete a 5k run without walking some of the distance. My goal was to run, without walking in the race, no matter how slow I ran. And I knew I would be slow.

Four weeks later, I was at the starting line. All I could think of was running. First was the swim, then the bike, and the run was last. The order was the best thing going for me. By the time I got to the run, I would be too invested in the race to quit. I would force myself to finish — no matter how much pain I was experiencing. I was more afraid than before I started training. I didn't have a fancy carbon fiber prosthetic, instead I used the same leg for all three events.

The race started, and I quickly realized I was not swimming a 500-meter swim. I was drowning in a lake, next to 300 hundred people. Everyone was fighting for position. I thought, "These people are serious! This is intense!" The swim took me 14 minutes, not a terrible time. I seemed to be in the middle of the pack. I didn't know if I was exhausted or exhilarated, my adrenaline was pumping. The element of competition was much higher than I anticipated. It was exciting.

Next up, the staging area and on to the bike in a hurry. Who practices getting on their bike in a hurry? The bike took me 52 minutes. I fell behind the middle of the pack. The front of the field was flying. I saw people returning on bikes almost as fast as I entered the course. It was impressive to witness. It didn't take long to realize — I need a different bike. I came off the bike tired, but I enjoyed the experience.

The run was looming in my mind for the entire bike ride. The closer I got to the end of the course the more afraid I became. I got to the staging area, off the bike and the 5 kilometers (3.1 miles) awaited. Within the first mile, it seemed everyone was ahead of me. It was obvious that my residual limb was sweating profusely. I could feel a raw blister. The prosthetic limb I had was not made for running. It felt like running on a brick. The impact hurt my left side, up to my hip. I pressed on. I said to myself, "I am not quitting, no matter what. And I'll finish on my own terms — no walking." That was my way to finish strong. The strongest, slow 5K finish, in 48 minutes. But I didn't walk a step, and I did it my way.

When I did my first triathlon in August 2009, I learned a lot about myself. The sores on my limb alone were enough excuses to quit. When something is hard, there are always reasons not to finish. Maybe it is smarter not to finish. Some say, "Triathletes are crazy and risk serious injuries. Or triathletes risk a heart attack in the middle of the race. It's not worth the risk." Sound familiar? Frequently, people tell me they worry about my health, because I push myself.

In March 2010, I moved to Georgia for business reasons. My wife and our five small children remained back in Bay City, Michigan. I was coming home almost every weekend. I was thinking about the triathlon race and I really wanted to do it again. When I was in Georgia, I didn't have time to train. I returned home in September 2011, and I was presented with the opportunity to buy into Bremer Prosthetics. The intention was to purchase their Saginaw office.

During the transition, I didn't work out as much as I used to. All my hours were spent opening my new office and growing the business. When I considered doing another triathlon, I knew I was overweight and old, so I dismissed the thought. My wife noticed my melancholy mood and encouraged me to start water skiing again. I liked the idea and knew I would have to get into shape. I felt with all my responsibilities, the only way I could commit to working out, was if I tied it to work. I wanted off the excuse track, so I shared my frustration with my business partner — Nate Kapa, also a certified prosthetist. He encouraged me to do the Sanford and Sun triathlon again in July 2018. We had a plan — to create awareness for amputees. We would make a specific prosthetic leg for each tri event and use it to market our business.

Long distance running was the only event that made me feel limited in my physical abilities, as an amputee. I could play basketball but sprinting up and down the court was not the same as long distance running. Eventually my limb would sweat, and when it did, the friction started, and pain began. When playing basketball, I could stop and dry off. In a race, I couldn't carry towels and rubbing alcohol with me. I wanted to see if I trained to run long distances for seven months, could I condition my limb to handle the socket environment? Could technology like vacuum suspension help minimize friction? I was going to commit to the one thing I didn't fight for after my accident — running. I began running 24 years after my accident, at 48 years old.

I trained for a month before I told anyone what I was doing. It was real in my head, but saying it aloud meant I was committed. I started running in March 2018, with a specific plan. I ran half a mile at a time. I stopped, rinsed my leg with rubbing alcohol and ran again. I gradually increased the distance my residual limb tolerated. Nate would make me a new socket each time I lost weight. At first, I lost 20 pounds and the prosthetic limb didn't fit properly. We continued redesigning the prosthetic limb for the race. By June 2018, I lost 40 pounds and we made final adjustments to my running leg. It was empowering to run on a prosthetic limb that was designed for running. I never had one before, and I felt better than I did in the last 24 years. It was funny though — I was hoping I might gain some competitive advantage as I heard — but no such luck!

As I continued to train, I set goals. My body and mind were changing. In June, I ran 5k, not for distance, but to increase my speed. I began to rethink my limitations. I was out of my comfort zone, challenging myself, and experiencing growth. The development of the mind through training, is more advantageous than the physical benefits. Once the mind knows excuses are unacceptable, the mind adapts to what is possible and accomplishes the task. My goal was to finish the race in less than one hour and 30 minutes.

People approached me about running with a prosthetic limb and make a variety of well-intentioned comments. I recall a time when a woman watched me run on the treadmill. When I finished, she pointed at my prosthetic limb, "That is amazing." I replied, "This does not run by itself, the human mind is amazing." Another time, I was approached at the college where I worked out. "Look at you swimming, running, and working out just like everybody else." The week of the race, a man said, "You inspire people every day, and you don't even know it." I thought, "I am not doing this to inspire anyone." The man went on and continued to tell me that he lost weight and finished his first triathlon last week. He said he would wake up in the mornings and not want to work out. When he went to the gym, he saw me training and thought, "Why should I complain when another guy is doing it with one leg. You helped motivate me." I was glad to be a part, helping him get to the finish line. I saw him at the Sanford and Sun two years in a row. I re-defined what I was doing. Up to that point, I thought what I was inspiring amputees. If someone lost their limb, they could find hope for a full life by watching me.

The day of the race, I was anxious. Nate raced with me. I felt tired during the swim. The plan was for me to change my prosthetic limb at every transition. I had one for swimming, one for biking, and then one for running. Changing the legs took longer than I thought — I didn't practice that part. My swim time was 12 minutes. I was on the bike and back in the transition area in 42 minutes. Then on to the run for the finish. I crossed the finish line with an overall time of one hour and 32 minutes. Two minutes from my goal, I was disappointed. I worked hard to achieve my goal and I came up short. I contemplated where I went wrong and where I could improve. I'd rather miss by a little, then reach it by a lot and feel unfulfilled.

I raced in the Frankenmuth, Michigan triathlon the next weekend. The way to practice staging, is to keep racing. Afterwards, I was approached by a spectator, who watched the race. Her dad had a leg amputated recently, and she was inspired watching my accomplishment. I smiled — that was what I set out to do! I realized that I stood out while doing that. I didn't know who I could impact, but when anyone is inspired, I've accomplished my mission. I adopted a new saying:

It doesn't matter if you have two legs or one leg.

You can always find reasons not to do something.

It's what you do, that defines who you are.

In October, I raced again, "Tri for Mac," McKayla was an amputee, in the prosthetics program at Eastern Michigan. The race was sponsored by the prosthetics department at Eastern, and as a prosthetist and amputee, this was big. I knew Mckayla — and the race was inaugural.

A year later, I competed in the Sanford and Sun again, July 2019. Casey Quinlan competed with Nate and me. Casey was an amputee who worked with me at our clinic. Watching him finish his first race inspired me. I finished in an hour and 24 minutes. That was the best I felt after a race since the beginning. To top it off, my 5k time was 28 minutes. I gained speed and ran in a way that I never thought possible.

Later, I realized that I have become comfortable. I'm ready to get out of my comfort zone again and challenge myself more. Next year, I plan to do an Olympic distance triathlon and run a half marathon. Where there is a challenge, there is growth.

If you are looking for change and want to grow — challenge yourself with competition.

Give it a TRI.

.

Determined to Succeed

Maggie Rettelle

I was training. "In training" has lasted for years now. I set my goal to qualify. To be good enough — to show myself and the world — who Maggie Rettelle really is. For six years I held that goal in my head. Six years of competing in three IRONMAN® races. And it finally happened in Chattanooga, Tennessee. In Chattanooga, all my training paid off. I qualified for the IRONMAN® World Championship in 2019.

It was one year until my goal race. Training continued. On a Sunday in early September, everything changed. I completed the end of a well-executed workout weekend. I was deep into my run. I kept myself around a 7:15 pace. I felt invincible. I was fit and ready to compete against the best athletes in the world. I ran on the city sidewalks keeping my pace and managing my footing. This was familiar territory and I was aware of my surroundings. As I passed an apartment complex, I saw a red sedan approaching and it appeared to accelerate. The driver was heading straight towards me. I reacted quickly, pushing myself off the front, side panel of the car to avoid being hit. I ran home feeding off the endorphins of my work out. I remember feeling sore that evening and attributed it to the hard work I put in over the weekend.

The next day, I felt sharp pains in my pelvis and all the way down my right leg. I was limping and couldn't fully extend my leg. By the afternoon, I was in so much pain that I left work and scheduled a chiropractic adjustment to get realigned. The adjustment reduced my pain from unbearable to a level 9, out of 10. I was then able to hobble. Sleeping was excruciating. Each time I shifted in bed I awoke from the pain.

I went to work limping and grimacing. The ibuprofen helped to reduce the pain. I decided to swim thinking that the compression of the wetsuit and non-weight bearing exercise may relieve some of the pain. But a storm blew in, and I was unable to do an open water swim. I rearranged my workout plan and jumped on the bike. I only lasted for 25 minutes. I sat on the bike, and the pain and tightness in my hip and hamstring was too much.

Strong-willed to swim, I went to the pool and did a 1300-yard test. It felt amazing. The weightlessness and movement relieved some of my pain and gave me hope for healing. After another chiropractic appointment and deep tissue massage, some of the pain was alleviated, and a bit of mobility returned. My new focus was on full mobility. I was determined to heal quickly. Swimming was where I found the most relief, and so I swam daily.

There was a week of swimming and adjustments. I was becoming more flexible and started to walk normally again. It was time to try biking. I could sit comfortably but not in an aero-position. The back of my leg was tight, but I could maintain a decent power level for a 45-minute ride. I continued swimming, my weakest discipline. I embraced the challenge and worked harder. I appreciated the opportunity to push myself more and see improvement. I didn't think that way in my previous swim workouts.

Sitting became more bearable for me over longer periods of time. I also had a drastic range of motion improvement, following another deep tissue massage. My focus on other tasks enhanced, and that helped me shift my tapered training focus. I channeled my energy into organizing cupboards and closets. I call it "pre-big race nesting." The rest from training also provided me time to make an itinerary for Kona, Hawaii.

Training continued with swimming and biking. I listened to my body about when to add the run back in, to avoid feeling pain. I struggled to maintain my happy face, and so I worked to maintain health and contentment. I had five weeks to get to the starting line. During that time, I spent hours swimming, I biked as much as my body allowed, and ran minimally. It was never as much as I wanted to do. I spent money I did not have and time I could not afford — to get well. I realized that I am human and not invincible. But I was determined to succeed. I knew I would make it to the starting line. The next step, traveling to the venue in Kona, Hawaii.

The flight from Denver to Kona was a long seven hours, without much opportunity to get up and move. My partner, Chris, and I had aisle and window seats, in case the flight wasn't full, then we would have an extra seat. But that didn't happen. The woman in the middle seat, Jean, and I introduced ourselves. I asked her if she wanted the window seat, and I would sit next to Chris.

About five hours into the flight, I asked Jean if she wanted to get up and stretch her legs or go to the bathroom. She said "No, that's alright, I'm like a camel." I liked her immediately. We continued with small chit chat. We talked about nutrition and getting old. We talked about her life, working at the police station. And I helped her figure out how to work the entertainment system on the back of the seat. We also talked about my race that Saturday. She said she would check it out and perhaps try to watch it. I gave her my cell number. We said some cordial goodbyes as we got off the plane.

I got a text from Jean on Friday, and she said she was staying right at the exact turnaround of the race. She told me she would be watching. Jean planned to make me a sign, "Go Maggie Go!" She was so excited about the race! I thought it was so cute — the amount of effort she put into a perfect stranger who she met on a plane.

Race day was hot! The bike course was hilly, and it was windy from the turning point of Kawaihae up to Hawi. Unfortunately, the power on my Garmin failed, and I had to go by pure feeling. I knew that the bike would be the slowest bike ride ever. I decided to enjoy the experience. The winds picked up and started swirling and blowing me across the entire road. Often, I rode out of aero position, to assure safety and get optimal power up the hills. I was feeling tired and hot after 50 miles.

I started to think about Jean. Was she really going to be at the turn around? I thought about only having 50 more miles to go after seeing her. It helped to click the miles off and keep my focus. And then I saw the sign!! But no Jean?! Another woman, whom I found out later, her sister Betty, was holding the sign. I yelled to her, "I'll be back!" I went on to complete the infamous turn around in Hawi. I got back and went the half mile down the road to find only Betty sitting under a tree, holding the sign. I stopped and asked, "Where's Jean?" She said, "She went to the bathroom." "No!!!" I exclaimed! "After all the excitement and time she put into making her sign and spectator plans, she won't get to see me." So Betty, (probably an 80-year-old-woman) went trotting back into the house.

As time was ticking, I had a decision to make. Do I wait for Jean? Or do I just get back on the road? I reevaluated the past year and my journey to get to this spot in the race — my goal race. Yes, it was a race. But it was also a journey with different paces. I thought of many people who made a difference throughout my journey. At several points during the adventure, I stopped to express thanks to my family, my friends, and my support system. Jean was a new member of my team. It was then that I made the decision to show my gratitude. While I waited, I took the opportunity for a quick stretch of my legs and my hip, which were feeling the familiar tightness. I knew I was tender from the last five weeks of recovery, and I was hopeful it wouldn't get worse on the run.

Suddenly Jean appeared! She literally ran to me. A 75 plus-year-old-woman ran to me as if I was her long-lost daughter she hadn't seen in 10 years! She grabbed her sign and yelled, "Go Maggie, Go!" We snapped a quick picture, and I was off again. Her smile was priceless. I grinned ear-to-ear, the rest of the way down the hill. That moment gave me the inspiration I needed for my last 50 miles on the bike ride. I returned to transition and headed out for the run. I completed the race knowing my biggest fans were waiting for me.

It took all the focus I could muster, each day, to get me to the starting line. The positive attitude I maintained throughout my treatment, aided in my recovery. I pushed myself within limits to heal, quickly. I had no more time. I had to make it to the finish line. I have worked for this race for seven years! I started the journey when I was at my worst, out of shape, abused, divorced, and sad. My former partner tried to hurt me by telling me, "Your running will never get you anywhere. You're not an elite athlete."

However, I completed six Boston Marathons and the IRONMAN® World Championships. I am content to have reached my goals. I am a survivor. I persevere. I plan to strive for more when the challenges become even greater.

Thank you — to Chris, my family, my friends, and my new support-team member, Jean!

An Instrument of His Work

Michael DuCharme

I lay in bed, taking in the news, with the phone still in my hand. The call I received was from Susan, the nurse practitioner (NP) for Dr. Mike, my Oncologist at U-M Hospital. "Michael, we have the results from Thursday's surgery, the nodes we removed from your thigh were negative for cancer activity." News that surely should have set me free, took several weeks to register.

After the holidays, December 28, 2011, I was heading back to work. As an avid runner since high school and college, I finished my morning run and showered. I sat on the edge of the tub, to put my socks on, when I felt a sharp sting on the inside of my right leg. Above my ankle was a mole, about the size of a fingernail. It didn't have the usual dark brown color, instead it was black and raised. I headed next door to my neighbor and ex-wife, Becky, to get her opinion. She took one look and said, "You'd better call Jane to have that checked." Jane was both a close friend and our family physician. I explained I was waiting on a call from her office.

When Jane's office called, the nurse asked, "What's going on Michael?" After I described the mole, she put me on hold for a few minutes. Upon returning she said, "Maybe you aggravated the mole somehow. We have you scheduled for your annual physical in January, a couple of weeks, we can check it out then." The mole continued to stay in the back of my mind.

Even though Becky and I were recently divorced, we had a good relationship. But what was about to happened between us — a nurtured friendship — was something neither of us would have predicted. Her father, Frank, was in failing health and would be gone within a few weeks. I suggested that she visit him after work, and I would take care of walking the dog and feeding him and the cat. Her father passed just before the holidays.

The days before my scheduled physical were especially stressful at work. In the world of radio sales, it doesn't matter what your past record is, it's always "What have you done (sold) lately?" The only thing worse than not selling anything is to have a client cancel an order. That's what happened — two clients cancelled their schedule, the same week. This led to a meeting with the sales manager and the Vice President, to go over my account activities. It didn't matter I was salesperson of the year, twice. They just wanted to know my plan to make up for the revenue.

While at my physical, the nurse checked my vitals. Despite being a runner, I still had high blood pressure. The nurse shared my concern, "Michael, you are 160 over 91. Is that a white-coat reading?" Boy, I surely wished it was. I didn't want to go into details of the stress I was under. I shrugged my shoulders and said, "Probably," but from the tone in my voice, and the look on her face — neither of us were buying it.

Jane greeted me and immediately wanted to see the mole. After she took a closer look, she asked, "Mike, you're not going back to work after this, are you?"

"Oh yeah, I'm heading back. Why?"

"Can you give me an extra thirty minutes? I want to remove that mole and have it biopsied."

I could tell by the look on her face there was concern. "What are you thinking Jane?" I asked.

"I want to send it off to be biopsied." I pressed on for an answer, "Come on Jane it's me...it's melanoma isn't it?"

"It looks like it, but we're going to find out for sure." As she washed her hands she said, "If it is, I'm sending you to U-M. I promised myself that my next patient who faced this, I'd send to U-M, where they have a Melanoma Clinic. Not that I have any issues with the specialists in this area, but that is all they do there."

It turned out to be a huge blessing to me. After she finished my physical, a nurse came in to prepare my leg for the mole removal. She called me the following Monday and said, "Mike, the biopsy shows it is positive for metastatic melanoma. The margins are clear. However, I am sending you to U-M where they will take a football-like section of skin from your ankle until they are confident it's all been removed. My office will contact you to set up the appointment."

I don't really remember the rest of the conversation. I couldn't get over it. In my mind, I kept repeating, "You have cancer. You have cancer." I received the call the next morning for a consultation appointment at U-M. They strongly suggested that I bring a second person with me. Both to help retain the information and to ask the doctors additional questions. Without question, Becky agreed to go.

At U-M, we were introduced to Dr. Mike, an oncologist surgeon and Susan the NP. Jane was spot-on with her description of what their surgery would be like — a football-like incision, removing additional layers of skin until they reached clear margins of their satisfaction.

Then Dr. Mike added, "However before we do that procedure, we are going to have you go down to radiology. They will shoot blue dye into your leg, where the mole was, so we can find the location of the nearest lymph node. After we have reached clear margins, we will make a small incision, remove the node, and perform a biopsy to determine if the cancer has traveled."

A node is the size of a pea that has a vessel attached to it and carries lymph fluid — a clear, watery liquid that passes through the nodes. As the fluid flows through, cells called lymphocytes help protect the body from harmful germs. Dr. Mike said that it could be in my groin area, or behind my knee.

I haven't had surgery as an adult. So, I was naturally curious how the procedures would affect my muscles, my running, and my recovery in general. I was told that recovery would be fast, and I must keep clean dressings on both incisions and protect them while showering. Going back to work would not be a problem.

My surgery was on Valentine's Day. Everything went as planned, except the surgeon found two nodes near the skin's surface, instead of one. Both were plucked for biopsy. Three days later, I received a phone call from U-M with results from the inguinal procedure. "The first node was negative for metastatic melanoma. The second node showed rare, large cell activity, consistent with metastatic melanoma tumor cells."

"What exactly does that mean?" I asked.

"You have cancer...I'm sorry," the doctor replied.

I couldn't think of a more gut-wrenching, bitter way to face my mortality, then to hear those words. I know the conversation continued with next steps and who to call, but the only three words I heard were, "You have cancer."

I was back in Ann Arbor the following Wednesday when Dr. Mike shared with me three options: 1. Do nothing. Although the cancer traveled, it was minimal, and my immune system could possibly take care of it. 2. Go into a clinical trial where I had a 50/50 chance of either being observed or receiving an inguinal dissection (the entire node pad from the groin removed).   3. Go through the standard inguinal dissection operation.

While Dr. Mike explained my options, I was on the exam table and Susan was checking out the small incision made to remove the two nodes from my leg. She informed Dr. Mike that the sutures inside my incision broke and needed to be repacked.

Susan called Becky over and explained how to pack the incision. At that point I spouted, "What is packing?" Susan explained, "It's a long piece of gauze like this," and she held a thin piece about shoulder-length long, "soaked in saline solution. And placed into the incision where it heals from the bottom up."

I quickly inquired, "Can I watch?"

Susan stopped, looked at me for a moment then asked, "Are you going to pass out on me?"

"I don't think so," I replied.

She lifted me into a sitting position and said, "Have a look."

I leaned over to look and immediately understood why Susan asked the question. I sat there, looking at my incision, and instantly, a queasy feeling came over me.

Susan assured me it would heal in a few weeks, and eventually Becky wouldn't be able to pack much gauze in it. Before we left Ann Arbor, I made up my mind with option three. The surgery was scheduled for six weeks later. Becky suggested I move into her guest bedroom to make it easier on everyone.

I decided to run during the six-week waiting period. I was worried about the effect on my leg muscles and my overall performance.

Would it slow me down? Would I have less power in my right leg? Would I develop lymphedema? In addition, I biked to build leg strength. I managed to get some exercise daily.

Three weeks later, Becky packed the incision one evening. "Michael, I can't get very much in there." After only three weeks, there was concern. I called Susan. She paused before responding. She asked, "How much gauze is she able to get in?" "About half an inch," Becky chimed in. Susan immediately replied, "Wow. It sounds like you're done. Put a bandage on it and let me know if anything changes. I'll see you in a couple weeks, before your surgery." That gave me confidence to continue to surgery, in the best running shape possible.

Surgery day arrived and I felt confident in the outcome. Susan explained the procedure, "Surgery will take approximately three hours. We will probably have to move some muscle to get to the node pad and close the incision with several staples."

As I was being wheeled into the operating room Becky gave me a long squeeze on my hand, smiled and said, "I'll see you in recovery."

Sure enough, when I woke, Becky was there. Through all the ups and downs, she remained by my side. Susan stood behind her. "Michael," she said, "everything went extremely well. You were in surgery for an hour and twenty-five minutes. They did not have to move any muscle to get to the node pad. They closed you up with sutures."

I said, "But you told me it would be three hours, and they would have to move muscle and close with staples. Why the changes?" She replied "Michael, we see about two people like you per year. You are in excellent shape, especially for your age. Most patients your age have health issues, and many are obese." I thought to myself, "My training paid off."

Yet I stared starkly at my mortality. In my younger days, I felt so sure of myself... so in control. As I got older, suddenly things were not so black and white. Was the cancer gone? Would I be able to regain my running form, my speed? Would I even be able to hit the roads again? Would the surgery leave me physically scarred? For most of my life I've been the "glass is half-full" type of person. What I felt as I began my recovery was anything but that.

The medical terminology for it is Post Traumatic Stress Disorder (PTSD), usually associated with soldiers returning home from battle. I simply called it depression and I was absolutely scarred as hell of the battle I found myself in. Once again, I was in the care of Becky, staying in her spare bedroom. She was incredible and supportive — I don't think I'll ever be able to properly thank her for her kindness, compassion, and yes — her love.

One morning, as I cried with fear of the unknown, I decided to turn to *God* for help. I began my covenant by saying, "All right. I'm going through this even though I have no earthly understanding of why. But if you help me beat this, I promise you, that I will devote the rest of my life helping people fight their illnesses. Please God, hear my prayer, in your name I pray, amen." It wasn't a lavish request. It was a short, and to the point, desperate prayer for help.

Then Susan called the next day, informing me that they had the biopsy results. They found five additional nodes in the pad that were removed, and they all were negative. I thanked her and we said our goodbyes. I lay motionless with my phone still in my hand. The cancer was gone. I thanked God for hearing my plea.

A few years later, in 2010, I ran the Boston Marathon. I was 58 years old and decided that Boston would be my last long race because of the toll it took on me. But for some reason I still felt the urge to run a marathon. The Chicago Marathon was on my bucket list. I went online to register but it was closed. Then I noticed at the very bottom of the home page: *Run the Chicago Marathon for Charity.* I clicked on the link and found St. Jude listed as one of the charities. I knew it very well. Comedian Danny Thomas started the hospital. As a kid I used to collect old newspapers, recycle them for money, and my mother sent it to St. Jude. The money helped children and their families fighting cancer and other deadly diseases.

The timing couldn't have been better to call. "Hello, St. Jude Children's Research Hospital, Lynette speaking, how can I help you?" I told Lynette why I was called, and she said, "I have one spot left, would you like to sign up?" Without hesitation, I took the spot. My life was about to change, forever. I signed up at the Gold Level which meant I committed to raising $3,000.

We may never understand everything that happens in our lives — I certainly don't. Yet, I firmly believe I was meant to have that bout with cancer to bring me into the St. Jude fold.

Today as a "Heroes Ambassador" for St. Jude, I recruit other athletes to raise money through their races. It ensures families of the children at St. Jude, never receive a bill for treatment, travel, housing, or food. To date, I have raised over $30,000, thanks to the generosity and kindness of many friends and relatives who have helped me keep my promise to God. Although, I can't take credit for any of it because I am *an instrument of His work*.

If Darkness Comes,
TRI Something New

Frank Szostak

I have always been an active person — from snowboarding, rock climbing, motorcycle ice racing, to scuba diving and cliff diving. Some would call me an adrenaline junkie, and the summer of 2012 was no exception. I was active in the sport of motocross racing from 2008 until 2012. Motocross was an activity I shared with my son, my girlfriend, and her son. With everything I did, I always looked for ways to get better and be more competitive in my age group.

In July of 2012, my motocross race season was going great!!! I was riding a new bike and feeling very confident with my abilities. On a beautiful summer day in Northern Michigan, some friends and I were riding a new motocross track, nicknamed Red Bud of the

North. It was a very challenging track, almost pro-caliber. I took a few warmup laps to get a layout of the track. As I completed each lap, I found myself increasing my speed, and pushing further. The last jump of the track was just before the start/finish line, and I had not cleared the section yet. I thought to myself as I approached the section, "I'll need more speed in order to clear it." As I hit the face of the jump, I turned the throttle a bit more.

There are times in life, when we wish we could take back some decisions we've made.

On that day, the decision to throttle-up was not the right one. I hit the gas at the base of the jump and felt the front end of my bike rise straight up. I launched through the air and stood upright on the foot pegs. Immediately, I knew my jump angle was way off, and there was no time to correct my landing.

I landed on the other side of the jump — like I was on a pogo stick. My rear tire struck the ground. My body weight compressed down on the foot pegs, and a burning sensation shot through my lower back. Then my feet flew off the foot pegs. When the front tire struck the ground, I was in superman position — my legs straight back, my hands with white-knuckles gripped the handlebars, and my arms fully extended. Only by the grace of God did I manage to ride out the landing. The bike and I fell to the ground. I was on my hands and knees struggling to catch my breath. The next few seconds seemed like an eternity, as everything was silent.

The silence broke moments later when the track rescue crew shouted, "Are you alright?" It's funny to think back. I am sure I said, "Yes, I am fine." I attempted to get up on my feet. "Fine" quickly faded and was replaced with the fiery sensation in my lower back. With every attempt to move, the sensation shot right through me. Being on all fours seemed my best choice. I was assisted into the track crew cart and taken back to the pit area. I could sense that a hospital visit was in my future, the burning sensation was there to stay. Into the back seat of my buddy's truck I went. I tried to remain on my hands and knees as we headed to the hospital. It was one hell of a ride.

At the hospital, I was placed on a backboard and taken into the ER. For what seemed like hours, I was questioned, examined, x-rayed, and finally given some pain meds — which barley made a dent! When the doctor came in with my results, he informed me that I had a severe compression fracture of my L1 vertebra. On the x-ray, my vertebra looked like a wedge of cheese.

I was presented with the options, and I settled on the conservative approach. It was a reality check when I was told that I would be in a full back brace (turtle shell), from my waist to my neck, for the next six to nine months. My life drastically changed. From a decision I made, doing something I loved. I lived by the credo: *If you play hard, sometimes you get hurt.*

For the next several months, my time was spent walking and laying around. My scans indicated that I was healing ahead of schedule, and the doctor wanted me to increase my activities. He suggested low-impact exercise such as swimming, and I started visiting the local pool. I have always been athletic, but swimming was hard for me. During my trips to the pool, I met a few people who were training for a triathlon, and they encouraged me to give it a try. They were more than willing to help me develop my swimming skills, and with each pool visit I felt confident and stronger.

I had a newfound passion developing. My motocross days faded with the realization that I was a lucky individual — and it was time to find a new activity. Finally, I was out of my turtle shell back brace, and back to running and swimming. My older brother was also going through a tough time, and we found ourselves spending more time together. We decided to train together and signed up for our first sprint triathlon in Lansing, Michigan. We bought bikes, gear, and committed to a training plan.

Finally, race day was here. Did we train enough? Could we hold our own? The anticipation, the build up — and then poof, it's over —

brought back feelings of Christmas morning. In the blink of an eye, I finished in the top 10 of my age group. What a rush. The adrenaline junkie in me was hooked on something new. Since that day, I've competed every year, racing in three to six events each year. I have been very competitive in my age group, landing on the podium in most races. I transitioned to the Olympic distance in 2016 and competed at the USAT Nationals in Cleveland, Ohio in 2018. Continuing to push myself, I committed to my first, half Ironman event in June 2019.

With the guidance of my multisport team members who competed in the half distance Ironman, I began training eight months before. The commitment was big, and I was all in. I had the full support of my best half, Jamie, who understood what it would take. She encouraged me on the days I just couldn't find the energy to train. She even joined me on bike rides and swims. Now, I've met a lot of great athletes during my seven-year journey, becoming a triathlete. Not one of them made it without a strong support crew. My success was no different.

Month after month: eat, sleep, swim, bike, run — repeat — week after week and month after month. That's the triathlete life. Training was going great. My confidence was high. My "real" life was also going on. My daughter was receiving her master's degree from Wayne State University on May 2, 2019. To say I was a "Proud Daddy" is an understatement.

Graduation day arrived. Jamie, my Mom, and I were headed to meet my daughter for her big day. I felt as if I was on cloud nine, hitting on all cylinders. But as I learned a few years earlier, things can change on a dime. We left home and were about 10 minutes into our trip. I was doing some work on my phone, while Jamie drove. My concentration broke suddenly, as I heard the words, "OH FUCK!" Quickly, I looked up to see a flash of red (the van), a loud crash, then a total whiteout (the airbag). It is true what they say — tragic events occur in slow motion.

To this day, the seconds that followed still pass slowly through my mind. We were hit head on. I looked at my mom, laying on the back seat with blood on her face. She was alert. I looked at Jamie, in the driver's seat. She was still gripping the steering wheel, startled, but otherwise okay. My focus shifted back to myself as I struggled to breathe. Each breath matched a severe pain in my left rib cage.

The unknown was a scary place to be. I was in that place. No matter how hard I tried, I could not catch my breath. Jamie came around to check on me. I was concerned about notifying my daughter, who expected us at her graduation. That was not a call I enjoyed making. The moment broke as the sound of sirens filled the air. Rescue personnel were on the scene. I was prepared to be removed from the car. During the process, I was hit with the all too familiar burning in my lower back. My thoughts flashed back to the decision I made, which ended in the same burning sensation. I was strapped to a backboard, and we were off to the hospital.

I lay in the emergency room, staring at the lights. My mind was running a race of its own. I didn't hear from the doctors yet, and my thoughts were in high gear. "What about training? What about the half marathon Sunday? What about the June half Ironman? What's wrong with my back? How's mom? How's Jamie?" When my x-ray reports came back, the results showed signs of severely bruised ribs, and a fracture to my L5 vertebra. Further testing was scheduled. I was holding onto hope that the testing would come back negative. My injuries would be limited to bumps and bruises, and my race season would continue.

Follow up tests were completed, and pain meds flowed freely through my veins. I lay waiting for the Neurosurgeon. All my hopes and prayers could not have prepared me for the conversation that followed. The doctor approached my side and placed his hand on my shoulder. He jumped right in, "Mr. Szostak, you have a fracture to your L5 vertebra. Your recovery is expected to take six to nine months." Once the words left his mouth, I was overcome with emotions. Tears streamed down my face. I trained my ass off. The race was snatched from me because of someone else's decision. I tried to reign in my emotions. The neurosurgeon leaned forward and softly said, "I am a marathoner, and I was sidelined by injuries in my past. You are in very good shape, which will help your recovery. Take time to heal and live to race another day."

His words were a blessing. A silver lining in the dark cloud that engulfed me.

Six days later, I was released from the hospital with a back brace, a walker, and a supply of pain meds. I was a prisoner in my own home. The week before, I was free to swim, bike, and run to pursue my quest in my first half Ironman. Friends and family were supportive, but the visits slowed down, and time slugged on. I tried to stay in touch with my training groups, but discovered that being a spectator at events, felt worse. I heard the saying, "Idle hands are the devil's workshop," but never dreamed I would be plagued, with thoughts of suicide.

Normally, I was a positive person, and I can't recall negativity in my world. Yet, I was tormented by my thoughts. Over and over my mind would spin. I lay in bed at night, knowing that next to me, in the nightstand, there was something that could end it all. And lying next to me was my best half — a woman so supportive, so loving, and so giving to me. But I couldn't share that with her. I couldn't be seen as weak.

The control I had of my life, was taken from a person who crossed the centerline. I was lost, without direction. The thoughts were intermittent at first, then consumed my days. I tried to share these thoughts with a few close friends. My attempts to self-analyze provided some relief but my mind always returned to the control I had over my life that was taken away by the person who crossed the centerline, but I was alive. I found myself visiting this dark place more often and pulling myself out was getting more difficult with each passing day. Much of my daily routine had changed. I was lost with no direction the day my thoughts drove me towards action. "Get up and clean it," ran through my head. "If you use the gun, at least it will be clean." I sat outside on a beautiful sunny afternoon, and I thoroughly cleaned the "thing" that could end the dark thoughts. When I finished, I realized what I did. Quickly, I removed the clip and secured it in the lock box. That night while getting ready for bed, I told Jamie where I put the gun and key. That was me calling for help — but not loud enough. Her reply was, "Okay."

I failed to scream at the top of my lungs.

When I realized that these thoughts would kill me — literally — I found my way onto a counselor's couch. It didn't take long for him to inform me that I was suffering from Post-Traumatic Stress Disorder (PTSD). Week after week, we discussed my thoughts, and how the accident played a big part. He pointed out that my personality was one of being in control and competitive. When that was taken away, I didn't have the skills or experience to combat it.

I have never done anything half-assed. I have always been in it to win it. So, when my counselor recommended, I try something new, I was in. He suggested I start doing daily walks, without paying attention to my pace. "Don't look at your watch." This was a difficult task for me. All runners know that our pace is the gauge we live by, to show improvement. I needed to improve. The walks lead to slow runs. The idea entered my head that maybe, just maybe, the doc will clear me in time to participate in Nationals. I was already registered and raring to go.

Also, I was attending physical therapy three days a week. I was cleared to swim, but biking and running were still restricted. Maybe it was my competitiveness, or my stupidity, but I started riding a bike and stretching my runs out. I continued to wear my watch, but I only checked it for distance, not time. I drastically downplayed my daily activity when questioned by my physical therapist. No, I wasn't a good patient at that point. But the dark thoughts faded. Things looked brighter. I thought of salvaging my race season and participating in Nationals.

I shared my plans to compete in Nationals in two weeks with my best friend. He had one question, "Has your doctor cleared you?" What was I going to do, lie to him? Paul was never one to hold back his opinion, and this day was no exception. In simple terms, he said, "You're not cleared, which means you're not 100% healed. What happens if you crash your bike and land on your ass? Is participating in the race more important than being able to walk? I'm not pushing your ass around in a wheelchair."

The question, "What if I crashed?" never entered my mind. I was so consumed with getting back to my tri lifestyle, that my desire to compete blinded my thought process. The Cleveland trip changed, and I spent race day without risking my wellbeing. Instead I basked in the Florida sun with the most important people in my life.

Finally, I was cleared for full activities, early October 2019. I began training again, for my first half Ironman in June 2020. I plan to complete my other goal, a full-distance event, when I am 55, the Louisville IRONMAN®, in October 2020.

The journey I traveled over the last six months was a ride I would wish on no one. But it was not a wasted trip. I realized that I don't have to win every race I enter. It is okay to enjoy the ride!!! I still have the desire to be the best in my age group, and I accept if I'm not. From one triathlete to another — when darkness comes calling — TRI something new. You never know where it will take you.

The Day We Made Lemonade

Branden Scheel

Where do I begin? My girlfriend Alexa, her family, and I woke up in Longmont, Colorado at 2:45 a.m. We left the hotel at 3a.m. We dropped transition bags in Boulder, Colorado and made our way to the reservoir to get set for the race. When we arrived, we got our body markings and went into transition... then the fun began.

I walked up to my bike and noticed that something wasn't right. It rained the night before, and I covered my handlebars and seat, but my handlebar bag was missing. I thought it was just the wind, and I unwrapped my seat. As I walked in towards the transition area that morning, I realized the incline. I thought I should move over one more gear, so it was easier to pedal when I began the bike leg of the race out of the transition area. I clicked my Di2 button, to shift .... nothing happened. I had electronic shifting, which were little electric wires and a battery that shift for me. The electronic shifting needs the battery charged regularly. This Di2 shifting was a great thing to have in most instances, but when there was a problem, it was a big issue. I checked the connections and tried shifting again. Nothing. Perhaps water got in my battery somehow, and it shorted out. At the time, I thought that would probably be the worst-case scenario.

Immediately, I took the bike to the technical support tent and explained everything. They thoroughly ruled out possibilities — like an old battery, or batteries not charged, etc. We did not have a charger to run diagnostics, but the tech guy said he was 90% sure it was a shorted-out battery. Without a charger, we couldn't know for sure. They did not have a backup battery or anything else to help me, at that point. I prayed hard that something good would happen. On my way to the announcer's tent, I ran into Bonnie, who was simply the sweetest person ever. I asked her to pray hard for something good to happen, and to have an incredible day, in case I didn't. I rushed over to Mike Reilly in the announcer's tent and asked him to announce that we were in need of a charger.

While I sat waiting, I called my parents with the bad news — either I needed to borrow one of their mountain bikes, or I wouldn't get to race. I also helped Alexa get ready for her race, but we were both furious and in no mental position to prepare. As we prepped her bike, the bike techs found a spare charger in one of their cars! We ran up to a generator and plugged the bike in. Nothing happened and an error reading came on. "Yup, the battery is shot," he said. I started to tear up thinking my day had ended before it could even begin. But something told me to try again, to try a couple more times. Error reading.... then another error reading......then CHARGE LIGHT!!! This meant I had power. We tried shifting the bike, but nothing happened. He double checked, and confirmed I had full power in the battery.

We went back to the tent and continued to look for the problem. He thought it could be the wires, inside the bike, around the crankset that were missing a connection or got wet. So, he pulled off my crankset, bottom bracket, bottom bracket shell, and pulled out the wires from there. I could tell he found something, and he asked, "How competitive are you? Like, are you competing today?" I thought that was a funny question and replied, "We are all here to compete today!" He asked a little more sternly if I was competing for a Kona spot, and I said, "Absolutely." He looked me in the eyes and said, "Well someone tried to stop you — because this wire was cleanly cut."

I stared in disbelief. He showed me the clean cut, and right in the middle. It was put back to make it look normal, so I would never notice. Furious, frustrated, and sad — a mix of emotions came over me. I asked what he could do. We came up with a plan: not to have a front derailleur so I could have a rear. I would be stuck in a 55 tooth chainring all day (one of the biggest used on the road). It meant the hills would be brutal, but at least I had a chance. We would have to re-route the whole bike, tape the battery to the outside of the bike, and hope it lasted for five hours.

He began setting it up, and I called my parents with the news. It was 5:45a.m. and the races began at 6:05a.m. It was going to be tight. I began to fill my water bottles, and he finished the final touches just as they called to close the transition area. For some reason that day, I took a sip out of my bottle. I never do this but for some reason I did. An AWFUL taste hit me. I spit it all out and tried again. Same awful taste. It was like the WarHeads sour apple spray had been dumped inside of my bottle. I told Alexa, just to confirm, and she said she could smell it from a distance. WHAT THE HELL?!? I rinsed out my bottles three or four times and filled them with the proper liquid. Then we headed to the start line. Because time was tight, I didn't adjust my bike back to the way I like it. The seat was not angled right, nor was the seat post right. If I wanted to do the race, I had to get to the start line immediately. I didn't know how the day was going to go, but I was going to finish the damn race.

I still fumed with anger as I reached the swim starting line. I took a deep breath — it was time to compete. I used my anger to fuel my day. I raced a conservative, but good swim at 1:07. I swam alone, near a few other guys.

Transition went well and I hopped on the bike, chilled to the bone. For the first few miles I just sat pumping my legs, while my body shivered. The air was barely 50 degrees and my speed was around 23mph, I was absolutely freezing. I held great power and found my groove. With the derailleur stuck in the 55 tooth chainring, I knew I needed to conserve some energy for the three big climbs of the course.

I headed into the first climb, and it was not too bad. I joked with a few racers as I went up and it didn't faze me. I rolled along holding great power and came to the second climb. Legs frozen and fingers not working right, I knew it would be a challenge. That one required 400 watts for around 45 seconds, just to get up the hill. It took a huge toll on my legs, as I aimed to stay around 180-200 watts that day. I took off on the downhill and saw my family! Dad gave me splits to my age group competition, and everyone's cheers kept me going strong.

I came up to the third and final hill of the first lap. It was brutal. It was a gradual increase in incline and kicked me in the face at the end. I got up to almost 500 watts just trying to stay upright on my bike. I continued clicking my shifter and hoped there was another gear, but it never came. I reached the top and used the next three miles of downhill to recover. Although I was fueling and pacing great, the hills were too much for my big ring in the front. But I pressed on to lap two.

I started lap two with one goal: conserve energy, so I don't have to walk the last two hills. I was REALLY starting to feel the incorrect bike position. My hips were pinched, my knee started to hurt a little, and I felt shooting pains in the side of my ankle. I backed off my power. I forced myself to hold back and made sure I ate enough. Around mile 60, I warmed up and everything started to feel better. I came to the first hill and got up with just a little fatigue. I used the downhill to heavily reduce my watts and recover. I came to the second hill. I told myself, "Just two to go. Two really Fu#*@ing hard minutes, and you can recover for the last 15 miles." I approached the hill, and I asked my legs for one more minute. They did not have much of a kick in them, but they made it up the hill. Slower than before, but they made it! Again, I used the downhill to recover, I took some nutrition and deep breaths. I saw my family again, which I needed as my legs were starting to feel the giant surges.

ONE. LAST. HILL. I came to it knowing that would be the hardest part of my day. I started up the hill, asked my legs for one last minute. There was nothing there. No answer. I literally screamed out loud in pain as I climbed the hill. Nothing left in my legs, 95 miles in, and I begged my legs for everything they had. I crested the hill and let out a big scream. I also cried a little because I was happy. I made it, and I was done with the hills. I did not pedal for almost two miles after that. I had nothing left. For the following five miles, I coasted and pedaled easily, just trying to get home. I was over being on the bike, and I didn't care about anything other than getting off. The last few small hills felt like they tripled in size. I struggled to climb. I slowly crept into town and made it to transition. 4:57:44. Good enough for today!

Now for the "run." I came out of transition and my legs felt weak and unstable. I took a few steps and my hip began to hurt. I knew I was in for a long run. For the first few miles, I ran and jogged, but around mile three, the pain became too much. I walked basically from mile three to mile 26. Miles three to six, I tried to run at least a quarter of each mile to keep my times decent. By mile six I was having no part of the running thing. I decided to just get my money's worth of food and beverages on the course and had a one-mile picnic, 20 times! At each aid station, I grabbed Coke, Gatorade, cookies, pretzels, chips, grapes, and I munched until the next one! In addition, I made it my goal to say something positive to every single person I passed, for the next four or five hours. Just because it wasn't my day, didn't mean I couldn't help make someone else's day! I cheered loudly and hard for every amazing person around me. Walkers, runners, limpers, and anyone in between. Positive words do wonders, and everyone could use them, no matter their speed.

I pressed on, eating, cheering, pumping people up, and limping inch by inch, foot by foot, mile by mile. I saw Dad around the corner. I was waiting and hoping for him for a while, and he walked with me for a bit. I told him my racing day was over, but I would be an Ironman later that day. I just wanted my money's worth of time on the course. It was nice having the company and he told me Alexa was just a couple miles back, so I would probably see her in a few miles. Mom also walked with me for a mile and we talked about the day, and she kept me company as I continued. I gave her a hug before heading towards the halfway mark. I continued my goal — cheering every single person, eating as much as possible, having a blast with the volunteers, and joking around all day long.

At the turn around, a medic asked how I was doing. I told him some Ibuprofen and Tylenol would be life changing. He told me all he had was infant aspirin. I said, 'Load me up!" I walked while he made sure the dose was right, and when I returned, he asked if I was a pro or trying to get to Kona. I said not a pro yet. At that point, Kona was nowhere to be found, even if I were to skip the whole second lap. He informed me that taking the meds made me ineligible for a Kona slot. I responded by asking, "So how many can I get?" I was focused on finishing then. Hopefully with a little less pain — no Kona, no winning — just finishing. I confirmed I was not disqualified, only ineligible. He said, "correct," and I downed the baby aspirin quickly. Off I went!

I saw Alexa at the turn around, about 1.5 miles back and gave her a big hug and kiss. I calculated I needed to go a little faster, if I wanted to have a chance to make it to the finish line with her. I thought it would be super-cool since we both had off days. I decided to run a little bit. My watch was set to give me splits every half mile, so I decided I would walk 0.4 and run 0.1., which was all I could manage. I kept this up until mile 14, and my hip slowly started to loosen up. I stretched it to 0.12, then 0.15, even got to 0.2 miles. But each time, I was shut down by the pain. I had some watermelon and jogged a little more. I came up to a table on the side of the path, and yelled out, "RED VINES?!?!?!?!?!? I LOVE RED VINES!" The lady at the table laughed and said, "Take them all!" I revealed an evil grin and said, "Don't tempt me. I still have a three-hour walk. I will kill'em all." She promptly switched to, "Take a handful." I agreed and walked off, in heaven.

I walked the following two miles, cheering hard for those around me, and I saw my family again. I gave them hugs and continued my beautiful walk! A little later, I saw someone familiar run by, it was Sam, who I coached a few times in cycling class! I caught up to him. I felt good enough to run with him for a while (thanks, baby aspirin) and we talked. We chatted about our days and helped each other along for the next three miles. My hip acted up again, so I sent Sam off to become an IRONMAN®. I rooted for him as he ran ahead.

I knew I was finally far enough ahead, where I could meet Alexa at the finish. It would be a blast and a decent end to our not-so-great day. I saw Alexa at the turn around again, and she slowed down. I gave her another hug and kiss before heading to the finish...slowly. I still cheered for every single person as I made my way to mile 23. I saw Dad again, and he said, somehow, I was in 4th place, and if I wanted to be on the podium, I probably needed to jog in! Honestly, this was so far away from my mind. I was completely over the podium. I just wanted to finish with my girlfriend, which meant more to me than a sad, 4th place. He told me she was just behind me. He ran back and jogged with her until they reached me! We walked/jogged together for the final two miles. Until we achieved the most memorable finish I could've asked for. A couple of rough days came together, as we shared an incredible moment — crossing the line together. Because hey, when life gives you lemons.... lots and lots of lemons...

That day taught me many things. It taught me to roll with the biggest punches. To pray when life gets hard. It taught me to fight harder. To look for solutions, not excuses. To finish what you started, no matter what it takes. And most of all, to laugh. Even in the hardest times, find happiness. My marathon took me 22,000 more steps than usual. It was more painful than anything I had ever done. But I did it. I walked/ jogged/ hobbled 54,467 steps to be an IRONMAN® again. It was a day to remember, no matter how it started. It ended with victory, in my mind. A moment that I will never forget.

A Gradual Progression

Jennifer Brown

I'm a 38-year-old mother of two boys, and I'm married to an amazing man, Pete. I was born and raised in Mid-Michigan. My story is of a gradual progression and love for the sport of triathlon.

In 2016, I weighed 298 pounds. I knew I needed to make a drastic change. I have always been on the heavy side, but my weight really spiked in my 20's and became worse after having kids. Hearing the doctor called me morbidly obese, while I was pregnant with my second child, really struck a chord. Family members told me that I could be pretty, if I lost weight, which hurt even more. I didn't think beauty was defined by size. It seemed easy for someone who never struggled with weight, to judge others. It wasn't easy for me to be heavy or to lose the weight. I tried for years. I worked out twice a day, swam before work, and lifted weights afterwards. But I never got below 250 pounds.

After giving birth to my second child, I struggled with postpartum depression. I ate my feelings. I gained 20 pounds following his birth. I knew people who had bariatric surgery, but I wasn't sure if it was right for me. I discovered that my local hospital had a monthly bariatric meeting. I signed up for the meeting the following month, even though I already knew what I wanted. I showed up with the paperwork filled out.

A few weeks later I met with the doctor, and he agreed that the sleeve would be the best option for me. With the sleeve, 80% of the stomach is removed, which means hunger is not really experienced. In order to have the surgery, I had to meet with a dietician, once a month for six months. I was evaluated by a psychologist, had a stomach scope, and lots of blood work. After meeting with the dietician, I learned that I would be irreversibly limited in what I could eat after the surgery. I'd never be able to eat more than a half cup of food at a time. Carbonated beverages would be a thing of the past. I'd also have to give up rice, bread, and pasta (my favorite food). None of that stopped the show.

In the months leading up to the surgery, I didn't tell many people my plan. I told my parents and in-laws right before the surgery, and I swore them to secrecy. I didn't want others to judge me, it wasn't their business. The day before my surgery, my mother-in-law called me, and tried to talk me out of it. I hung up the phone and cried for 30 minutes. That call filled me with doubt. While I know she didn't mean any harm by the call, I was in a fragile state.

The surgery went well. I woke up in recovery and it hit me like a brick to my face. I had five incisions, and the biggest one hurt the most. It was equivalent to my c-section. It hurt to lay down, get up, or do anything. I wore an abdominal belt for six weeks after my surgery.

Along with the post-surgery pain, there were huge changes. I had to drink 60 grams of protein a day and 60 ounces of liquids — all in small sips. I would sit and sip all day in order to get my liquids in. It took me weeks to get up to the intake I needed. The liquid diet lasted a few weeks, and then I was able to move on to pureed foods, which was heaven after a liquid diet. I only ate a couple spoonsfuls and I was full. With clearance from the dietician, my diet progressed. Finally, I was able to start exercising, and I chose to swim again.

I swam in middle school and high school. On the first trip back to my local pool, I got in 1800 yards, which felt amazing. I started swimming three to four days a week. I noticed the weight fall off, and I increased my distance each workout, each week. I averaged six to nine miles and lost two to four pounds a week.

Then I added running. I started talking about doing a 5K race, and how I'd love to do a triathlon one day. My husband started looking online at races for me. He found one that was local to us, an aquathon. It was hosted by a local multisport club, Team ATP. I practiced with another member, Nancy, since I never swam in open water before. It was a completely different experience than swimming in a pool. I only made it a few hundred yards before I wanted to turn back. Nancy was super-amazing and took me back to shore.

Immediately, I purchased a personal swim buoy from the club as a security blanket. Nancy told me that they meet weekly for open water swim practice and encouraged me to join them. I showed up the next week and met more members of the club. Linda and Bob invited me to swim with them since they both knew that I had no idea what I was doing. That time, I made it around the entire course. They talked me into coming back the next week and every week until the August race.

To say I was nervous on race day would be an understatement. It was a Wednesday night race and I was a ball of nerves while at work that day. My husband and kids watched me race, which was amazing! I started in the back of the pack with Linda and Bob. I jumped in the water, and I was off. I got to the beach and ran into the transition area. I took my time putting my shoes on because I didn't know the time counted toward my overall time. I finally exited the transition area and started running. At that point, my running was weak. I had to walk for a few seconds here and there to catch my breath, but I finished. Crossing the finish line was huge for me. That was something I wanted to do for a long time, and I did it. I was 80 pounds down at that point and I felt amazing! That was the only race I did in 2017, but I was pumped to say the least. I know it wasn't an IRONMAN® — but from where I started — it felt like it.

I swam with Team ATP through the fall, winter, and spring. I went to the spring 2018 Team ATP event, and officially joined the team. I was excited to have something to train for. My open water swim practice led to a better time than the year before. Linda and Bob provided me with encouragement, valuable advice, and talked me into doing a triathlon.

The super sprint was a local race at one of the beaches I used to frequent as a kid. My husband, Pete, and Bob both showed up to cheer me on that day. This was my first big race. I was the first one out of the water. I ran into the transition, threw on my running shoes, grabbed the bike, the helmet, and ran out to the six-mile course. I came back in from the bike to see Pete and Bob near the transition, cheering me on. I ran the mile run portion and came down the chute to the finish.

It felt incredible to cross the finish line, and I felt that I could accomplish anything. I received my first medal, which I proudly wore the rest of the day. Shortly after receiving my medal, I learned that I was the first person across the finish line. That meant I beat 30 people in the super sprint division. I found Pete and Bob, and they asked how I felt. I told them I felt amazing and thought it was easy. Bob laughed and asked what I was doing the following weekend. There was another local race. I went home and signed up!

The next week flew by. Bob picked me up and we went to Frankenmuth, Michigan. The cool thing about that race was diving off a boat. Also, the start was staggered, which was nice for us newbies. I dove into the water and then game on! I swam at a nice steady pace to the turnaround. The bike ride was hotter than blazes, but I peddled on. I made it back to the transition area once again and set out for my run. At the start, it was over 80 degrees outside and climbing. I ran and then walked when I needed to and started running again. I was walking around the 3-mile mark when a few other runners came by and picked me up. I joined them and we ran the next mile together.

Then I stopped for a quick break, but after 20 seconds, I decided to keep running. As soon as I saw the chute, I picked it up and ran as hard as I could. I came a long way from December 2016 to August 2018. I entered the Athena category and took first place for that group. I wanted more! We neared the end of the Michigan tri season, but there was another race that Bob suggested, on the ride home. We decided on a relay team for the Tawas race in September. I'd take the swim, he'd bike, and a friend would run.

Race day came and we received word on our way to the race, that the swim portion was cancelled. The water was choppy, and the mix of air temperature with water temperature created a bad situation. The weather can change in an instant on the Great Lakes and leaves no mercy. I wanted to compete and was relieved that they added a 1.5 mile run to replace the swim portion. I brought an array of clothing and was prepared. I started and finished my portion strong. Bob and Paige both rocked their legs as well. We came in second overall, in the relays.

After my first three races I knew I was hooked. I had to work on running. Linda suggested I start running with her and her friends, the Turtle Girls. They welcomed me with open arms. I started to run with them weekly and enjoyed it. They gave me pointers and information. I went from running 50 miles a month on my own to 100 miles with my girls. I worked toward my first half marathon in Kentucky, which doubled as a girl's weekend. I worked from home and running with the group was also my social time. Running with friends, led to the development of close relationships. There has been laughter, tears, and heart-to-heart moments on the runs. I've built lasting friendships with these ladies.

In 2019, I really stepped up my race game. I did six sprint triathlons, three Ragnar relays, two half marathons, and many other races. I completed my first marathon in January 2020, during the Walt Disney Marathon weekend. I did the Dopey challenge, which was four consecutive days of racing. A 5K, 10K, half marathon, and a full marathon. My friend Jenny and I trained for months leading up to this race — she couldn't get rid of me. We did back-to-back, double-digit runs, in late November and through December.

The weather prediction called for a very hot, full marathon. They nailed that on the head. Jenny and I ran the entire race together. It reached 90 degrees that day. We were on blacktop roads in the Florida sun for the entire race. Jenny brought us cooling towels, which we carried throughout the race. I went through 32 ounces of liquid in my hydration belt by mile 10, it was HOT. We were still moving well by the time we reached mile 22, but all the air was taken out of our tires and we were diverted. They had to pull medics from Blizzard Beach, due to people passing out along other parts of the course.

At that point, the course was red flagged, and we missed out on 1.5 miles. We finished the race and because it was my first marathon, I was determined to complete all the mileage. I left my medals and food box with Jenny and finished running my first marathon in the parking lot. Without doubt, that was the hardest race I've ever done.

Since having bariatric surgery, I feel like my world has opened. Not only do I feel good physically, but I feel good about myself. Before surgery, I didn't feel comfortable in my body. I felt anxiety going out to eat, not knowing the type of chair I would have to sit in. Being too big to sit in a chair is probably something most people have never had to think of. Once, I went to Cedar Point and couldn't ride a roller coaster because the safety harness didn't fit over me. I know that I never want to go back to where I was. I religiously stick to my diet and training to ensure that I stay where I am.

I look forward to many races in 2020! I really want to do my first Half IRONMAN®. I am planning several sprint triathlons in the summer, along with four Ragnar relays, and two more marathons. At times, I find it hard to balance my schedule with training, being a wife, a mother, a friend and with work. I am going in many directions, but my husband is my biggest supporter — I love that about him. I wouldn't be racing without his encouragement.

Ten Weeks After Open Heart Surgery

Brandon McDonald

Only ten weeks after I had open heart surgery, I completed the Draft-Legal Sprint Distance ITU World Triathlon in Lausanne, Switzerland. And this is my story.

It was a beautiful sunny day in Lausanne, Switzerland. I lined up alongside other triathletes at the starting line. My heart pounded with anticipation. I was surrounded by some of the best triathletes in the world. I knew I was there to do two things that day — represent the USA and finish the race. That race was different than other races I competed in. I attempted to finish the world championships only ten weeks after having open heart surgery. I stepped into uncharted territory. I was cleared by my doctor, but that did not guarantee that all would go well. I knew it could end in one of three ways: a miracle occurs and I finish the race, I start the race but drop out, or something goes very wrong and I end up at the bottom of the lake. One minute remained before the start, and I jumped in to get used to the chill of the water. The air horn sounded, my nerves were high, and I was off.

My journey to triathlon began as a runner. I ran most of my life, but eventually the wear and tear of my body caught up with me. At that point, I switched my cardio workouts to swimming, cycling, and running. When I started cross training, I didn't know much about swimming or cycling. I could only imagine what people thought as they watched me swim — they probably thought I was drowning. I watched YouTube videos and read online forums to learn and improve my skills. Then, I thought, "Why not try a triathlon?" I decided on the Grand Rapids Triathlon. That race was when I first saw an athlete in the USA uniform. I thought it was so cool and wanted nothing more than to wear my country's colors in a competition. Later, I researched the criteria to receive a USA uniform — qualify for the world championships at a national event, with a top-ten spot in the respective age group. That did not sound easy, but I resolved to train hard for nationals and reach my goal.

I put a plan together and began training. I could not get the USA uniform off my mind. A few months later, while out for a 50-mile bike ride, a car struck me in a hit-and-run. Miraculously, I crawled out of the ditch, called 911, and waved someone down. I was very fortunate that my injuries were not life-threatening. Slowly, I returned to training and maintained the progress I already achieved. The following summer, I competed in the Grand Rapids Triathlon for a second time, making the leader board and qualifying for Nationals in Cleveland, Ohio.

When I arrived at Nationals, I was disappointed to hear that the swim portion was cancelled. I did not run as much as I should have, due to a nagging IT band injury. I was confident the swim was my strongest asset. I placed 34th in my age group and didn't qualify for the world championships. I had one more shot. And I made the drive from Michigan to Sarasota, Florida, for the Draft-Legal

National Championships. I drafted only once, with a friend who taught me how to ride in a pace line. I was not quite sure what to expect of the race.

Before I left Florida, I heard of a possible hurricane forming in the Gulf of Mexico. It was projected to hit Florida around the time of the triathlon. The weather reporters were right, and by Monday it became Hurricane Michael, a category five storm. I contacted the park, and to my surprise the race was still on! I got out of work on Monday night, packed, and left within an hour. I drove 19.5 hours straight through, to beat the worst of the storm. On the morning of race day, an announcement was made — another duathlon — due to high levels of bacteria, the water was unsafe. I was disappointed because again, I hoped for the swim portion advantage. After all, I drove across the country for it. I gave it my best, and to my amazement, I finished eighth in my age group. I qualified for the 2019 World Championships in Lausanne, Switzerland.

In May 2019, I trained hard, made progress, and represented the Make-A-Wish Foundation at the Grand Rapids Triathlon. It was early Sunday morning, and I was out for an easy four-mile run before work. I glanced at my watch and saw my heart rate of 221 bpm. I blew it off as an incorrect reading, but soon after I felt a sharp pain in my chest, all the way down my arm. I experienced chest tightness, slurred speech, and a loss of sensation in my left arm. I finished my run but was worried the signs could be of a heart attack or stroke. I've never been a fan of going to the doctor, so I put it off and went to work.

The next day, I went to the pool for a swim to see if the symptoms would return. The lifeguard pulled me aside and asked if I injured my arm, because it flopped around in the water. My heart rate was still elevated, and I cut the swim short and went home to rest. I didn't want to miss a beat, so the next day, I went out to do time-trial sprints. I wasn't going to take it easy if I didn't "have" to. I wore two different heart rate monitors to check the accuracy of each. My heart rate remained within a normal range until the last 800 meters when it spiked to 210 bpm on one watch and 196 bpm on the other. When I saw the correlation, I knew there was a problem. I stopped my workouts until I saw a doctor.

A week passed and I finally convinced myself to get checked out. I went to the Meijer Heart Center in Grand Rapids, Michigan, because they were known as "cutting-edge" in heart health. The tests showed no sign of a heart attack or stroke — however they did discover a heart murmur. Then, I had a stress echo, which ended early due to my systolic blood pressure exceeding 250 mmHg. Other than that, it indicated normal results. The last test was a CT scan. When the physician's assistant walked in with the results, she looked very concerned and I knew something was terribly wrong.

She informed me that the CT scan showed a rare congenital anomalous of the right coronary artery (RCA). Basically, the RCA and LCA were positioned next to each other and twisted, cutting off blood flow to my heart by 50 percent and at another point by 70 percent. She explained the sudden death syndrome, where perfectly healthy athletes drop dead in competition, due to an unknown congenital heart condition. Most people with that condition experience sudden death in their 20s or early 30s. A heart catheter was required to see more and assess treatment or surgery. My case was presented to a team of surgeons and it was concluded that open heart surgery was the best option. As much as I didn't want the surgery, it sounded more appealing than sudden death. The most pressing question I had for the doctors was, "Can I still compete in the World Championships?" Their answer was, "Possibly, depending on recovery time and the amount of time required to train."

I scheduled the surgery quickly, to allow as much recovery time before the triathlon as possible. In the time leading up to my surgery, I researched healing aids, and fast recovery methods post-surgery. I found — the more fit one is going in, the faster one will recover after surgery. It was important to stay on top of nutrition with ample protein, vitamins, and minerals to help my body heal.

Just like building a house, if the nails or lumber are missing, it will impede the progress of building the house. I asked my cardiologist and was cleared to workout at a light intensity leading up to surgery.

In addition, I was warned not to push myself because it could result in sudden death. I continued with bike rides and told my family I was going for a short, easy ride. And I biked up to 24 miles a day, at a decent intensity. I made sure to keep my heart rate under 156 bpm. More than that, I could notice symptoms. I also maintained weight training, as my main desire was to have upper body strength, for the swim portion. Three days before my surgery, I stopped all exercise to allow my body to rest.

On June 18, 2019, I had open heart surgery. They performed a coronary artery bypass graft (CABG), which involved sawing my sternum in half and grafting an artery from my right mammary gland. They also clipped another blockage, made it a 90% blockage, and prevented it from impeding the blood flow of another artery. The days that followed the surgery were harder than I expected. While in the hospital, my family, and niece Kylie, visited me. It was a huge comfort having family there during such a difficult time.

My first walk was with a walker, to the end of the hallway and back. On day two, I completed one lap around the floor, then two laps, and then up to four laps. By day five, I walked up to two miles over the course of the day. As I was about to be released, my lung collapsed, and I had emergency surgery to fix it. Days later, I finally returned home. I remember looking in the mirror — I was as white as a ghost — like I was raised from the dead. The first week home, I barely had enough strength to do simple things. I regained my strength slowly.

A few weeks later, I went on a weekend trip with my family. I saw an indoor bike at the hotel. Curiosity got the best of me, and I had to see what I could do on the bike. At that time, I was not cleared for higher intensity cardio beyond walking. So, when everyone went to bed, I snuck down to the exercise room. I asked the guy at the front desk to lower the seat for me, because my chest was still healing. I rode for 15 minutes, at a medium effort, followed by a 10-minute cool down. Everything went okay, but it was hard to keep my heart rate down. Even minimal effort felt very difficult.

Once I was cleared to use the stationary bike, I added more structure to my workouts. I did anywhere between 50 and 70 minutes on the bike. By week five, I began attending cardiac rehab and my bike rides were close to two hours. There, I was introduced to upper body exercises with weights and resistance bands, to help regain strength. I used the resistance exercises to prepare for the swim. They simulated swimming strokes, sometimes up to fifteen minutes, to mimic the length of time in the triathlon. The cardiac-rehab staff was knowledgeable and encouraging. They helped me return to training quickly and reach my recovery goals.

Four weeks before the big race, I was on another weekend trip with my family. I went down to the hotel pool. Curiosity got the best of me again. I wanted to see what it felt like to swim. I took a couple of painful strokes and felt worried I wouldn't heal in time for the triathlon. A week later, I was cleared to run again. I ran two miles the first day, and it was harder than I expected. The following week — two weeks before Lausanne — I was cleared to swim. My first swim was 250 yards, and I experienced some chest discomfort. I rested for three days and hoped for improvement. I swam again, 550 yards, and still had chest discomfort. I chose to hold off on swimming until the race day.

It was hot and sunny in Lausanne, Switzerland, on August 31, 2019. It was a big day, and I put all my effort and energy into recovering for it. My nerves were high. The only thing on my mind was, "Will I make the swim?" I knew a miracle was necessary. Because I was in the last heat, it was likely I would be the last athlete to cross the finish line, in front of the whole world. That required a new kind of courage.

As I lined up at the start, I knew there was no turning back. I traveled across the world to compete in the ITU World

Championships, ten weeks after open-heart surgery. I put my cap on, my goggles on, and I jumped in. The water was chilly but crystal clear. The horn sounded and we were off. I tried to keep a consistent pace. As I approached the first buoy, I was still with the pack. I was thrilled, but then realized I should slow down and pace myself. I could feel the lactic acid burning in my muscles.

I almost wanted to drop out, but my mind jumped back to the time I got caught in a rip current in Lake Michigan. I surfed in November, and it was almost dark. I was swept out, past the lighthouse, where the waves no longer broke. I seriously thought it would be the last time that I would ever feel land under my feet — or see another human being again. I fought with all the strength I had and prayed to God to save me. Then, a wave came and carried me back into shore. I dropped to the ground and felt the cool sand on my face. I was exhausted, had nothing left to give, and I will never forget that feeling. I thought back to that moment, and I knew I had more to give and I needed to keep going.

I pressed on to complete the swim and experienced no chest pain. I was so excited when my feet hit the land! I gave a high five to someone from another country. I thought it would be all downhill from there, but I was wrong. As I ran into transition, my calves began to cramp. I made it onto the bike, and I tried my best to hydrate and relieve the cramps. The bike route consisted of many hills and long climbs. By the time I reached the next transition, I had very little energy for the run. The midday sun was intense, but I knew I could not give up.

I was exhausted, but I walked up hills, ran in the shady portions of the route and back down the hills. Finally, I saw the blue carpet and the finish line. The last stretch was a mix of pain, exhaustion, relief, and excitement. I gave my best sprint and crossed the line. I couldn't believe I completed the 2019 Sprint-Distance World Championships — ten weeks after open heart surgery! I truly experienced a miracle that day, and I give credit to God for all my success. I also want to thank my family, friends, and the amazing staff at Spectrum Health for believing in me and supporting me through my journey.

Drive to Succeed

Donna Heska

As I reflect on my life, I know where my drive to succeed came from. My drive to succeed exists in my marriage, my job, my triathlons, and everything else I do.

It came from growing up in a dysfunctional home. My father was a functional alcoholic, who physically and mentally abused me and my six siblings. I was raised on a large farm where everyone in the family worked long, agonizing hours, in all types of weather conditions: heat, rain, hail, sleet, and snow. Once, we were forced to hoe the fields during a tornado. My father thought he was making us tough. Thinking back, in a way my father prepared me for triathlons.

Transportation to and from the fields wasn't always by a truck or tractor. Biking or running to the fields was common. When there was a breakdown of the equipment, tools from the toolshed were required, which was at least a half mile away. It was up to me to get the tools quickly. I ran through the mucked fields. I didn't realize it at the time, but I was resistance running. I was making my legs strong for triathlons!

I endured a variety of physical pain during my childhood. I survived a smashed finger, with tissue exploding from both sides. A trip to the doctor didn't happen until the following day. My father ran over my legs with the potato harvester — not just once, but twice. Then I experienced blood poisoning in my right leg, from a horse accident. Along with several more traumas while living on the farm.

When I started high school, I was interested in team sports, especially basketball and softball. I tried out for basketball but didn't make the team. I was disappointed yet determined to make the team the following year. I begged my parents to let me go to basketball camp. I was the worst player at camp, but I continued to practice every day, after working in the fields. My determination paid off. I made the basketball team and was a starter for the remainder of high school. I was also a starter on the softball team.

My education advanced and I obtained an associate's degree in Applied Science, as a respiratory therapist. This was a stressful time: being a wife, raising my family, working full-time, and assisting in the health care of my father in his later years. Shortly after that, my life changed.

One morning, I tried to get out of bed and collapsed to the floor in pain. My lower body was swollen, and the pain was unbearable. I tried to continue with my life, but I couldn't move. I had to change my normal routine. My mornings involved crawling around the house and using support for at least the first 30 minutes of the day. Later, I was diagnosed with rheumatoid arthritis. I managed to continue to take care of my family and hold down my full-time job. I didn't dwell on my diagnosis. I thought of my grandmother, who had multiple sclerosis, and she never complained. She gave me the strength to move on.

There were days I wanted to give up, especially the days I had to take methotrexate, a chemotherapy medication. The prescription made me sick for four days with: nausea, fatigue, and weakness. I continued to take methotrexate as prescribed for 17 years, along with several different non-steroidal anti-inflammatory agents (NSAIDs), and steroid injections. I suffered complications, and I was diagnosed with cirrhosis of the liver. Even though I was highly medicated, I was not pain free. There were days the swelling and pain was so bad — I didn't think I could make it through the day. The constant increase and decrease of my medication to control my pain and swelling, took a toll on me physically and mentally. I was told that I had to cease my rheumatoid arthritis medications. I screamed as I reminisced about the pain, and the limited function of my hands, knees, and feet. I could not go backwards, I cried for days, feeling depressed and worthless. My family physician suggested that I get a second opinion.

After consulting with a new rheumatologist, we came to an agreement. My new therapy would include weekly injections of ENBREL. I saw an improvement after only one month. Three months later, I started running. I bought and followed *Galloway's Book on Running,* because it had been a long time since I ran. Six months later, I participated in my first 5K and a year later my first half marathon. The next year was filled with twelve races, including: 5K's, 10k's, five half marathons, and one full marathon. I felt so accomplished, but my rheumatoid arthritis was taking a toll. I hurt and needed to wear support bands during training and for each race. The pain in my knees was the hardest to endure. I knew I needed to make a change, but I wanted to keep up with cardio-activity. That was when I researched triathlons.

There was one discipline that could have been a barrier for me. I couldn't swim. I could float and doggy paddle, but not swim freestyle. I certainly couldn't complete a 500-meter swim. I worked on conquering my fear of the water. I took swimming lessons. I read books about swimming and watched DVDs and YouTube clips about freestyle swimming. I also have a severe fear of snakes, and I have seen snakes in lakes. That was an issue for the open-water swim. I continued to train.

I was ready for my first triathlon. I was so excited to finish the swim, especially knowing four months earlier, I couldn't even make it 25-meters without stopping. Once I was out of the water, I knew I could finish the triathlon — the hardest portion was done. I did finish, and I placed third in my age division. That was it, I was hooked on triathlons! That first race was a learning experience. I analyzed my swim, bike, run, and transition times. I looked at the data to determine how I could improve my times in each discipline. My fear of snakes continued to make the open-water swim training challenging. To this day, I still think about snakes each time I enter the water. At least I don't panic, I try to think positively.

I participated in six triathlons the first year, placing high in my age group and qualifying for USAT Nationals. Even though I was never pain free, due to my rheumatoid arthritis, I continued to forge ahead and forget about the pain. For 17 years before racing, I was fatigued and depressed from swelling and painful joints. Triathlons became my saving grace.

The second year, I experienced a setback at my first race. I struggled to swim effectively in the freezing-cold water. I had an asthma attack, and I could not catch my breath. I came out of the water as the second to last swimmer, and I was coughing up blood. I continued though, completing the 12.4-mile bike course. It was the hardest ride of my life. Still struggling to breathe, I started the run portion of the race. I used my inhaler. Instead of getting relief, my breathing became worse. At that point, I chose to abandon the race and seek medical attention. I was transported by ambulance to the local hospital and diagnosed with pulmonary edema. I didn't let this hinder my determination and went on to participate in my first half IRONMAN® and USAT Nationals again. That put the icing on the triathlon cake and motivated me more than ever.

In 2013, my goal was to complete another half IRONMAN®. I signed up for Steelhead, held in Benton Harbor, Michigan. While preparing for this race, I was biking and was hit by a F-150 truck. My bike and I were both beaten and mangled. Again, I was transported by ambulance to the hospital. I didn't have any broken bones, but I was very sore and had a bad headache. My whole body was bruised and battered. I was out of commission for a few weeks. I was determined to keep my schedule for a 50-mile bike ride from Harbor Springs to Mackinaw City. It was a difficult ride with my bruises still apparent.

Even though I experienced tragedies, I completed all the races that I signed up for. I placed either first or second. I also completed my second, half IRONMAN® and participated in the Olympic distance at USAT Nationals in Milwaukee, Wisconsin. It seemed that each year presented itself with both struggles and accomplishments. More recently, I have qualified for ITU World Championships two years in a row. What an honor to represent my country in both Gold Coast, Australia in 2018, and Lausanne, Switzerland in 2019. Both of those races were wonderful experiences.

As I look back at the tragedies in my life, I could have given up — and perhaps I should have. But I learned, early in my life, that quitting is not an option! My determination, willpower, and self-discipline has promoted me to become a successful TRIATHLETE and a better person.

Change Gears and Keep Going

Betty Bustrum

As a child, I was never introduced to any kind of sports — dancing, gymnastics and swimming, for example. I took summer swimming lessons for maybe a couple of years, then nothing.

As a young adult, I did absolutely nothing. I did not do any exercise on a regular basis until my late 40s and then it was walking the dog several times a week and gradually taking the dog on longer distances.

As I entered my 50s, I wanted to lose more weight from three pregnancies, and I decided to do more. I worked as an RN in a same-day surgery center and overheard several of my colleagues talking about how they rode bikes on the weekend. I told myself I could do that. So, I bought a hybrid bike and joined them on Saturday rides that involved leaving our town and riding along a riverbed to the beach and back. The distance was 25-30 miles.

The first Saturday I joined them was grueling and I could barely make it back home. We stopped 20 or more times so I could get off the bike and take a break. I was totally wiped, and it took days to recover. However, the more I rode the more endurance I built for longer distances. I persevered. I took the challenge. I felt good about myself.

I joined a local bike group and worked my way from novice to intermediate to an advanced level. Soon I was completing metric rides and centuries with that group. I met a woman and we talked about challenging ourselves. We thought it would be cool to do a triathlon even though I was a minimalist at swimming and running.

Several months later I moved to a different part of the state and sought another riding group. With a new partner we discussed challenging ourselves and she agreed it would be cool to do a triathlon. I was in my mid-50s. We decided to improve our ability to swim and run and take on an unbelievable challenge. Swimming was nearly impossible for me. I did not know how to breathe, how to move my arms or kick. Running was not much better. I was out of breath so quickly it was pathetic. I was discouraged and wanted to give up many times, but, once again, I stayed with it.

I worked with a swim instructor and a coach. I had workouts and tried my best to bring it all together. I signed up for my first triathlon. It was at the local YMCA and started with a 300-yard swim. I almost didn't make it. My coach was at the end of the pool cheering me on. I made it, did my ride, run and finished the race. I was extremely proud of myself. I could not stop thinking about my accomplishment.

Over the next year or two, I kept training and building my strength. I started signing up for mini-triathlons and sprints. Even the small distances were a challenge. Swimming was still my weakest link. Despite the coaching, open water events were especially difficult. During mini-triathlons with a 250-yard or more swim, I would often panic, stop at the safety boats and hyperventilate. With determination, I never had a Did Not Finish (DNF).

In my late 50s, I qualified for USA Triathlon Nationals. I felt so honored to do events. I enjoyed getting to know ladies in my age group who came from different parts of the country. The icing on the cake was at Nationals when I qualified to go to the International Triathlon Union Worlds. I was a woman without previous athletic experience representing her country. I was extremely proud of myself. I have had the privilege of competing on the Gold Coast in Australia and in Budapest, Hungary and Ponte Vedra, Spain.

I added a new challenge of a half-Ironman. I trained and thought I was ready to do the ride and run, even if I had to walk some of it, but that swim was very troubling. I made myself get in the water and I refused to be taken out by boat. I kept going no matter how uncomfortable I was. I have completed three half-Ironman triathlons.

In my early 60s, it was time for a new challenge— a full Ironman. While training my life changed in a heartbeat in September 2012. I was on a 50-mile bike ride that morning and less than eight miles into my ride when a fifth wheel truck and trailer hit me. I was unconscious when the emergency crew arrived on Pacific Coast Highway in Newport Beach. I have no memory of the accident or ambulance ride. I was transported to a Santa Ana trauma center and told I quickly regained consciousness. I remember being wheeled on a gurney back and forth from my room for CT scans all night long. They watched the bleeding on my brain, hoping it would subside and not require surgery.

However, I had several areas of my brain that bled. The left side of my head sustained a significant laceration and required staples. I broke my left clavicle and cracked my pelvic bone. There was a hematoma on the right side of my face due to the bleeding and significant road rash lacerations over my legs, arms and hands. While in the trauma center I had many x-rays, CT scans and MRIs to rule out additional bleeding and spinal injury.

With assistance days later I walked to the bathroom in my room. I remember looking at my face for the first time and did not recognize myself. My face was swollen and bruised, and around my right eye were all sorts of different colors. Every day a physical therapist would work with me while I used a walker. I was humiliated, discouraged and depressed.

After 10 days I was discharged, and they wanted me transferred to a rehab center. I was a nurse and stubborn and wanted to go home. They agreed as long as a hospital bed would be delivered to my house in La Quinta. I used a walker and a physical therapist would see me daily. I realize now that was a mistake. Even on oral morphine, I was in much pain and trying to make do with unbearable headaches. I could barely get off the hospital bed on my own and it was an effort even with the assistance of my husband. I had insomnia and small seizures, which I am told are normal after a traumatic brain injury. Due to my pelvic fracture, I ate while lying on my side.

Months passed and the full marathon I wanted to enter in November was fast approaching. I was angry that the chance to race was taken from me. I felt cheated because I put so much effort into training and could not do it. Getting through the holidays that year was hard. Loud noises and family activities were too much. I was easily fatigued. My balance was off and I continued to have difficulty walking. The headaches were still frequent.

I remember a visit with the neurosurgeon shortly after discharge and he said to my husband, "She should not be alive. At the very least, she should be in a wheelchair unable to walk." WOW! That was very disturbing.

A few months after my accident, there was a memorial in Newport Beach near where my accident occurred. A day after my accident, there was another cyclist who was hit by a car and she did not survive. The day after that another cyclist was hit by a drunk driver and killed. The city decided to have a memorial for cyclists and invited me to speak as an advocate for safe cycling. At the memorial I met the police officer that was the first responder to see me. He said, "I never thought you would have made it. I expected you to die." WOW again! The doctors felt that my being fit was a large part of the reason I survived. I was 63 and as fit as I had ever been before the crash.

Months later and deprived of my first marathon, I looked for a run that I thought I could do. I signed up and gave myself another challenge. I started training and discovered I did not lose all my fitness. That May I did my first marathon. Once again, I felt incredibly proud and wondered if I could do a triathlon again even though I could barely ride my bike. I felt overwhelmed and started to cry when cars passed. I could not do it with other riders. My friends found it hard to believe that I wanted to get on my bike again. Could I swim again? Could I do the running?

Just a year from my accident my friend started doing triathlons and talked me into going to Nationals in Milwaukee. She was going to do the Olympic distance, but I knew I could only do the Sprint. On race day, I was filled with anxiety. When the time came for my age group to take off, I started my swim and began to panic. A safety boat came and a person asked if I was okay. I cried uncontrollably as I clung to the side.

I got back in the water and started to swim. Soon I was hanging on to the boat again as the tears continued. The lifeguard said to me, "It's alright, you can get in." I said, "No, I am not going to give up." When I got out of the water, spectators cheered because they saw my struggle. I cried some more. I transitioned to my bike. I was one of the last ones there and a volunteer came to me and said, "Are you okay? Do you need help?" While crying I shook my head and mounted my bike. Halfway through I stopped crying. I did my run and crossed the finish line. Once again, I chose to get through it. A lady was at the finish line and put a finisher medal on me. I hugged her through my tears and she probably had no idea why I hugged her so tightly.

Shortly after that race I was diagnosed with a medical condition called PseudoBulbar Affect. PBA is frequently seen in people who have had a TBI. It can cause involuntary, sudden, uncontrollable episodes of crying or laughing and mine was the crying, triggered by anxiety. Doctors have told me it is a physiological problem that I may struggle with the rest of my life. It has affected my ability to continue with triathlons.

So I changed gears and decided to eliminate the swim and started duathlons (run/bike/run). I went to USAT National Duathlon races. As I said earlier, I was privileged enough to represent the USA at ITU events. I also competed in a duathlon in Spain.

I turned *70* in 2019 and it was a special year and *seven* years since my accident. I thought it was time for another goal, a half-Ironman and a *70.3*-mile biking event. Several members of the triathlon club signed up to go to Victoria, Canada to compete in a 70.3 and I entered as well. I worked hard on improving my swimming in a safe, indoor environment. I could do the bike and run miles, but I was unsure about my fear of water. I went to test myself in a low-key mile swim in Lake Mission Viejo. There was no pressure, no race, just training for open water swims. I was just going with my friends to a lake.

On race morning I was a basket case during a rolling start and I placed myself in the back with slower swimmers. As I waited my turn to enter the water, I became more and more anxious about the crowd and the noise. Almost immediately I started to panic. I couldn't get my heart rate down. I held on to the safety boat at one point and tried to take deep breaths and nothing worked. I got in a few more strokes and stopped. Another boat person came and asked if I wanted to stop. I asked if I could make the cut-off time and was told I could probably do it if I went nonstop. I didn't want to give up, but I called for the boat to take me out of the water. As the tears flowed, I felt humiliated, angry and defeated. I knew "the agony of defeat." I never had a DNF until then.

It took months to overcome the feelings of not finishing that race. Friends kept telling me, "Get over it. You will do another. You will come back next year, even stronger." I knew in my heart that I would not. I gave it my very best shot, but it was not and is not meant to be. My TBI emotional issues became too difficult to overcome.

Since then I have done two half-Ironman events as part of a relay. My strongest leg is cycling, and I did it first with my 19-year-old grandson and then with my 47-year-old son, three generations of us, before adding a relay with two ladies.

In a few months, I am doing another duathlon. I still swim, bike and run because I love to and because I can. It makes me feel good and keeps me physically and emotionally fit. I still set goals. I went skydiving for my 70th birthday. My accident has taught me to live life at its fullest and take on the challenges. I do not look back and say: "I should have, could have." Do not think you are too old. Be an example for someone.

Become Your Dream

Roseann Peiffer

My story began when I was a young girl. I was quiet and shy. Many of the adults in my life questioned my quietness at a young age, but my mom, being a teacher herself, knew I was just shy, and I excelled in school. In addition, my grade school gym teacher did not believe in me and thought I lacked athletic ability. She even asked my mother if I could ride a bike. I was one of the slowest kids when it came to the running tests. I was made fun of in elementary school. Perhaps, "bullied", which we hear so often today, was a more appropriate definition. As a young girl, my parents put me in swim lessons. I really enjoyed swimming, and I was always the last kid in the swimming pool, when all the other kids were getting out. My city's recreational center had a swim team for kids, but my elementary school released later, and my mother did not want me to leave school fifteen minutes early, to join the team.

Fast forward to middle school. I was involved in several extracurricular activities, and I finally joined a swim team in eighth grade. I enjoyed swimming and worked hard. So much so, that I was able to join the varsity swim team once I entered high school. In high school, I was recruited for the division three swimming, even though I never qualified for districts or states. When my high school swimming career was over, I cried — bawled, really. I had a hard time accepting the fact that I would no longer swim competitively. I decided not to swim in college and focused on studying. But I made a vow to myself to stay fit for the rest of my life, because I believed it was so important.

Even though my swimming career ended when I entered college, I took the discipline, dedication, and determination with me that I learned through the sport of swimming. Then I transferred it to everything else I did with my life. I obtained a bachelor's and a master's degree in exercise science, and even have my master's thesis published in the *Journal of Sports Science and Medicine.*

I remembered the fitness vow I made, and I started running to stay fit in college. I really did not like running before college, but I decided to go out and run two miles, no matter how long it took me. It took me 28 minutes that first time! From then on, however, I was hooked. I ran two to three miles, five to six days a week in college. And sometimes, I would swim and lift weights. I decided to train for half-marathons, and then ran my first full marathon when I graduated from college. However, I was not smart with my run training. I did not follow the 80/20 rule, and I was injured after my first marathon. I tried to train for another marathon, but again, I was injured halfway through the training. At that point, I decided to start cross training and training for triathlon. I remember watching the Hawaii IRONMAN® on TV when I was a kid and thought about how cool it would be to complete a triathlon.

When I finished my first triathlon and won my age group, I realized that I could be good at the sport. Plus, it did not involve as much running! Currently, I'm in my seventh year competing in triathlon, and I absolutely love it. I have learned a lot in the past seven years, and I have realized I have another strength in addition to the swim — the bike! I qualified for and competed in the past two ITU World Championship races for the Olympic distance. And I was ecstatic when I qualified for the 2017 IRONMAN® 70.3 World Championship, so I could take my shot at competing in a longer distance race, at a higher level. I was also on Team USA and competed in the 2019 ITU World Championship Grand Final.

I am living my dream of competing at a high level in sports. It has always been my dream to become a great athlete. I believe I have achieved that. My advice for others is — never give up on your dreams, and always believe in yourself. There will be people in your life that may tell you that you cannot do something. I have had my fair share of failures. What is important is — how we get up from the failures, dust ourselves off, and strive to reach even higher. Remember to be positive, and never, ever give up on your dreams. Become your dream, just as I have become my dream.

#forthosewhoc8n't

Jennifer Weber

My year of redemption was 2012. It was the year to regain "me", whom I lost during a very toxic five-year relationship. I decided at the beginning of 2012, that I would move forward with a goal to participate in one race, every month, every year — and it didn't matter what kind of race. The first, and probably the hardest, was a stair climb in the OneAmerica Tower in Indianapolis, Indiana. A short, 8-minute race, up 40 flights of stairs, which felt like an eternity. The pain in my lungs after that race was greater than anything I've experienced to date. Wow!

I continued my monthly challenge with a 5k run (which I never did before). I was a swimmer who HATED running, and I swore at my coach during dryland practice that I couldn't do it. I managed to run the 3.1 miles, an impossible that I turned into a possible. From there, I continued to build my running — five miles, and then a 10k. Someone convinced me to sign up for the Indy Mini-Marathon, 13.1 race. After I crossed the finish line, I swore I would never do a race that distance again. But the challenges continued, and the gratification of doing physical tests I once thought were impossible, was rewarding.

The following year, I went for a triathlon, to mix it up. Like 2012, I started small and built from there. In 2013, I completed my first Olympic distance race. I was introduced to a not-for-profit group called Tatum's Bags of Fun. The foundation collects backpacks full of toys and distributes them to the children undergoing chemotherapy treatments in Indianapolis, Indiana. It became my new purpose for running...for those who can't. The children suffered far more than what I would experience from the temporary pain of a race. That year, I completed my first 70.3 race. What I learned about myself, and the capabilities of my body through an endurance race, was amazing.

With the Tatum's Bags of Fun Team, I embarked on a new challenge for 2014, and wove in a financial goal. The challenge was my first full IRONMAN® event in Louisville, Kentucky. It was a very hot and grueling day, but there wasn't a moment that I forgot about the kids and that my pain was only temporary. I thought that the race would be a one and done. But the feelings I had when I crossed the finish line — pride, redemption, gratitude, and humbleness towards the sport — I knew it wouldn't be my last. I raised over $4,000 for the foundation and represented in my first 140.6.

Over the next several years, I focused on various race distances, from a sprint to 70.3, Half IRONMAN®. Four full IRONMAN® events later, I proved the first wasn't my last. After the second and third, I wanted to redeem myself from what I refer to as — the death-march-marathon — due to extreme heat. It was RECORD heat for those races. But that's a gamble to take with the long events. It's necessary to prepare for the best, expect the worst, and wiggle through the changes because you NEVER know what the weather is going to do. My times were respectable, but I wanted better. My most recent IRONMAN® in Arizona was going to be my last attempt for redemption. Not only was the sport physically taxing, but financially as well. I liked to say I'm, "in a perpetual state of Ironman debt." But of course, there were worse things to spend money on! Onward to Arizona.

I learned to check the weather, but not too far in advance. It creates anxiety and worry when it always changes back and forth. It can go from one day being cool, to a 50-degree increase, which I've seen three times! A week before a race, I checked the weather. It looked like it could be a PERFECT day. A low of 45 degrees and a high of 70. Can't beat that forecast. However, I still had the mindset to be prepared for anything. The mornings that led up to the race were rainy and cold. Not very desirable. The night before, the forecast remained as predicted, a light wind, which was important for that race, going into the desert. I have heard how difficult it can be on the B-Line highway with heavy winds. The morning was chilly, and wetsuit legal. As I suited up for the day, with my mom's help (I HATE wetsuits), I reminded myself why I was getting into this. I always reset my focus — I compete for those who can't. I was lucky to be there on that day, doing what God gave me the ability to do. I thought, "Thank you, Jesus, for this day!"

As I entered the water, I remembered to ease in and not take too deep of a breath. I didn't want to hyperventilate from the cold. Sixty-three degrees was chilly, even for me. The gun sounded, and we were off! I climbed out of the water one hour and seven minutes later. I made sure to keep my wetsuit ON for the almost .5-mile transition to the tent. PHEW that was cold. It was time to suit up for the 112-mile trek on the bike.

Never, have I had to wear cooler-weather clothes for an IRONMAN®. That time, I wore sleeves and a wind vest and much needed. The bike was a three-loop course. It was rough for a good two miles out of town. The day before, I made sure to drive a loop to assess the conditions and mentally prepare. There were several sections that had bad cracks in the road before the bridge, so I knew to look out for them. Once I was out of town, the course headed up the B-Line, and unfortunately got very windy. The headwinds slowed me down to 10mph at times. But coming home...was quite a rush! My highest speed was 38mph, without a challenge. Thank goodness the tailwind was on the way back. Loop one...success. The best part of the ride was being able to see my family several times. They were the best cheer squad on the Ironman circuit, for sure! Next, loop two.

When I reached mile 80, on the second loop, my race took an unexpected turn. Without warning, I flipped over my handlebars, projected my bike into the intersection, and skidded across the pavement. "HO—LEEY SHIT! What the hell just happened!?" My front wheel caught a crack in the road, and I went down. I had angels looking over me at that very moment. Only other athletes or official race support could help an athlete in distress. And one of the SAG guys, literally, was right behind me when I flipped. He rushed over to help me. I got up, my knee and elbow gushed with blood. I had a huge rip up the side of my kit and scratched my helmet. My chain was off and luckily, the SAG dude was able to put it back on quickly. He and another bystander were shocked that I even got up. I believe the exact words were, "That was a super-gnarly crash, not going to lie." SAG asked if I was ok and said medical was on the way. I immediately cried, "NO, NO, NO! I am NOT DONE with this race! Please don't let them come. I'm FINE, just let me go!" They asked me if I was 100% sure and I said yes. He told me that if I stiffened up, to PLEASE stop at medic. I promised.

"CARRY ON AND FINISH THIS BIKE DAMN IT!" I said to myself. I grimaced my way through the pain in my elbow, which rested on my aero pad. I had to make sure I smiled when I passed my family and friends. That was the only way they knew I was OK! One more loop in and out of the windy dessert. The wind picked up progressively, throughout the day. Somehow, I finished the bike just under a few minutes of a previous PR. My goal on the bike was to come off with fresh legs, and to RUN the marathon. I was never able to in the previous three IRONMAN® races — due to either extreme heat or cramping in my legs. Aside from the dried blood on my knee, my legs felt great. ONWARD TO THE RUN!

The weather was perfect for running, about 73 degrees and sunny. It felt warm at times, but it was GREAT in comparison to previous races. And it was going to start dropping as the day went on. That was when I realized the day I had been chasing after had arrived. I just needed to stick to my strategy: steady run, walk the aid stations, stay on top of water and nutrition, and especially electrolytes. I was delighted to find pickle juice at several aid stations. That should SOOO be a staple in all races. Tasty, and a wonderful hydrator. The course had several short rollers, which I continued to run.

Another two-loop run course allowed me to see my family, numerous times. It was a godsend. I messed up my watch in the beginning when I stripped out of my wetsuit, so I didn't know my total time. I did know — I was at LEAST on track to break 13 hours — which was my first goal. My second goal was 12:30, and my STRETCH goal was to break 12 hours. My father, around mile 16, with a bum knee ran alongside me for about a minute. He wanted to see how I was doing and informed me that I was on par for breaking 12. Another "OH SHIT" moment...really...ok... He said, "Don't get too excited, you still have 10.2 miles to go. Stick to the plan. Stay steady." My dad's words were what I needed to hear to hold on and keep going.

That day, I was doing the race for myself, to prove that I had it in me. But as the pain started to settle in, especially in my hip once I hit the pavement, I started repeating my mantra. "FOR THOSE WHO CAN'T, FOR THOSE WHO CAN'T. It's only temporary pain. Thank you, Lord, for this amazing day and the ability to BE HERE." As the sun set into the beautiful sky, I crossed the finish line for the fourth time. And I heard, "JENNIFER WEBER, YOU. ARE. AN. IRONMAN!" I reached a new personal record of 11 hours and 52 minutes. I could hardly believe it. I collapsed into the arms of a volunteer.

Immediately, I was taken to medic where they treated my injuries from the fall.

I proved to myself that — NOTHING is impossible. Even when we fall, when life is tough, we can always get back up, and redeem ourselves with pure will power and confidence. If it weren't for my family and friends, rooting me on from near and far, it could have ended differently. I owed it to them to cross the finish line, even if it took me all day. I will continue to shine and represent those who cannot. There are many others who commit to various challenges and feats in life — whether through a race or fighting cancer. Shine on, my friends! Continue doing what makes you happy each day and continue to bring smiles to others.

In the Silence of the Night

Scott Gayler

My headlamp battery was dead. My watch died hours ago. A seething, infectious darkness sucked all the joy and happiness from my world. I felt cold and isolated walking through the Canadian forest.

I felt more alone than any other time I could remember. I struggled to walk the last miles of my IRONMAN® race. The excitement faded, everything hurt. I was two miles from the finish of the race, but math was not on my side. Emotionally, I was drained.

The race cut-off was midnight and I knew I didn't have much time. I struggled to walk at a 20-minute mile pace. I felt like a complete failure.

In the silence of the night, a flicker of a memory came to me. From the edge of consciousness.

I was on the bus heading to the swim start.

When was that?

It seemed like a lifetime ago.

Was it really that morning?

It was!!! It started coming back to me...

* * * * *

There was a short walk to the bike transition area. I was escorted by an entourage of friends, almost a parade procession. Unfortunately, I was way too stressed and scared to enjoy it. I had a small list of things to do: get body marked, put running shoes and visor into my run gear bag, use my asthma inhaler, drop off my bike special needs bag, and get on the bus to the swim start.

Halfway through the bus ride I suddenly realized that I was wearing the visor that I was supposed to put into my run bag.

Crap.

I started the process of beating myself up...that was a stupid mistake! I just hurried through the morning. It was going to suck running without a visor, hat, or sweatband, but there was nothing I could do about it then.

I told myself it was a minor setback. Then I realized that I forgot to use my inhaler too.

CRAP!!!

That was an even bigger issue — it meant having to fight asthma attacks on the swim and the bike. I felt beyond frustrated at that point. Today was going to be incredibly difficult and I started it wrong. I had a second inhaler in my bike special needs bag with exactly one dose. I just needed to make it through the swim. I knew the cold water, the tightness of the wetsuit, and the heart rate spike of the start would exacerbate the issue...then I just needed to ride to the halfway part of the bike leg. On top of that, I looked and sure enough, I didn't put my nutrition in my bike special needs bag. I simply dropped the bag with my inhaler, a spare tube, and snacks but didn't put my actual fuel in the bag.

@#@^$!!!!

Hot adrenaline raged through my veins. I was ready to tell the bus driver to stop so I could give up. I spiraled out of control. By the time we arrived at T1, I felt the urge to curl up in a ball and cry. All hopes of a perfect day had faded. I simply hoped for survival.

It turned out that most of my mistakes were easily correctable. My bike nutrition was placed into a bag and put with the dozens of other bike special needs that were brought to the wrong site. My visor was given to a volunteer who put it in my run gear bag. I was still without my asthma inhaler. Not ideal, but I could control exercise-induced asthma in most cases, with a good warm up.

I found a place to sit down and get into the correct mindset for a long day.

One of the reasons I chose that race was because it was in Canada. Which meant that the national anthem would be, "O Canada". I didn't have an intense emotional connection with that song, I could hear it without tearing up. I was sure that if I heard "The Star-Spangled Banner" I would revert to a quivering emotional blob. Eventually, it was time to get into the water for the mass start. I crossed the mat and as my feet hit the water, something amazing happened. I had a moment of complete clarity. Everything that I could do to prepare for the day has already been done.

I only had three things to do now...swim, bike, and run. That I could do.

A hush fell over the people in the water, moments before the start. The cannon boomed. Within a few minutes, I found myself swimming with people going the pace I wanted. I saw the picturesque mountains that framed the swim. It was an amazing place for a swim. The weather was lousy all morning, but in the final lap, the wind and rain increased, doubling and tripling the amount of chop on the water.

As I approached the final turn, I nearly swam over someone who was struggling through the first lap. I didn't see until I was nearly on top of the person. I twisted sharply and my right leg seized into a cramp. My foot was locked, and I could not move my ankle. I mustered the willpower to swim a few meters outside the main flow of traffic. I tried to stretch out the muscle that cried in rebellion, but to no avail. One of the water support volunteers saw me and offered aid. I declined. They told me I could get out of the water to stretch and then continue. The cramp released, and I resumed the first leg of the triathlon. I exited the water at 1:13, on point with my optimistic projections.

I made my way into the men's change tent. The grass floor was turning to mud, the temperature was 40 degrees warmer than outside, and it started to smell like a teenager's unventilated bedroom. I dried my feet, put on my socks, shoes, and helmet, and made my way out of the tent.

I greeted my bike by name. With as much time as I spent with my bike, it seemed strange to not give her a name after all we've been through together. As we made our way, a new song started on the speakers. I knew the song, but I couldn't place it. I half-sang along, then it got to the chorus, "I like how it feels," by Enrique Iglesias. I ran with my bike and sang at the top of my lungs, "I like how it feels.... Ooh ohh ohh." As the music faded away, I heard the line:

"Take my hand, it's alright,
Cause' tonight we can fly."

I got on my bike in the cold, torrential rain but I smiled from ear to ear. When I made it to the highest point on the course, the rain turned slushy. I made the turn around and started coming back down the mountain. There were rivulets of water streaming down the road and standing water in places. I've rode enough in the rain to know my abilities. However, I didn't trust anyone on the road with me.

I consciously focused on staying relaxed through my upper body. I was extra vigilant for things that could be slippery and took care to avoid them, while also refraining from making abrupt movements. I periodically touched my brakes...not enough to lose speed but enough to make sure that my rims and brake pads remained reasonably dry. I also rode defensively, expecting the person in front of me to do the stupidest thing possible, luckily that didn't happen.

My wife doesn't like the idea of me bombing down descents. So, regardless of what my GPS watch has said, the maximum speed I go is 29.2 miles per hour.

So, I went down the 10-12% gradient at EXACTLY 29.2 mph, flying past riders who were riding their brakes. I saw people riding their bikes wrapped up in space blankets. Apparently, they handed them out at the bike aid stations. The blankets made a terrible rustling noise, somewhat like a baseball card in the spokes of a wheel.

Over the next hour the torrential rain showers faded to a sprinkle, and the sun even threatened to make an appearance but decided better of it. About 50 miles into the ride, I got my bike special needs bag which had my inhaler, a can of Pringles, and some other miscellaneous snacks. At the halfway point of the bike, someone had a stereo on a front-end loader tractor and blasted "Ironman" by Black Sabbath on repeat. It was appreciated by all. Then at the 70-mile point, I was singing "Living on a Prayer" by Bon Jovi.

> *"Woah, we're halfway there*
> *Woah, livin' on a prayer*
> *Take my hand, we'll make it I swear."*

At mile 90, I heard something "thunk" behind me. I nearly ignored it but turned and saw that my under-seat bag with my spare tube and CO_2 were ejected. I sighed, checked for traffic, made a U turn to get it, then another U turn and continued up the hill. The last 10 miles of the bike were climbing up a mountain pass and back to the ski resort. When I approached the final aid stop for the bike, the tube in my front tire exploded with a loud bang. Sigh, at least it was not raining. Plus, I got to use a floor pump from the aid station instead of a CO2 cartridge, and I could throw away the tube immediately, instead of carrying it to the next trash stop. I made my way to the end of the bike at 7:52. I hoped for 7:15...but with the wet ride and the flat tire, it was still a good ride.

As I stopped riding, the cumulative cold of the past few hours set in. I was freezing. Luckily, I had both a running vest, and a warm running shirt in my gear bag. I dried off, warmed up, ate a little, and sat in quiet dread of having a marathon yet to run. One of the volunteers shooed me away and I started the leg of the event that I dreaded with every fiber of my being. I began at a loping trot and knew that I had nearly seven and a half hours to complete that phase. It broke down to a 17-minute per mile pace, which was a reasonably swift walk.

The crowds were amazing despite lousy weather conditions throughout the day. Some were memorable, like the lady hitting the gong, the party of people along the golf course, the tequila guy who offered drinks to anyone who passed by — and took a good number of them himself. And finally, the cheer squads there for specific family and friends... but cheered for every racer as if they were family. Initially, that threw me for a loop, the people cheering for me by name, and I didn't have a glimmer of recognition who they were...then I remembered my name was on my bib.

About 10 miles into the run I thought to myself, "Anyone can do this, they just have to keep moving." I finished the first loop in about three hours. A reasonable run-walk combination. I got my special needs bag with my headlamp, which turned on in the bag and the battery was dead. That was when I started to mentally break. I had been racing for 12.5 hours. I started to feel sorry for myself. The fatigue started settling in. I may have been halfway through the distance, but I had slowed down. There were at least four more hours to go. I saw friends who were in the waning miles of their race. I was excited for them but wished with every fiber of my being that it was me who was almost done.

The run-walk turned into a walk-run and then devolved into a walk-walk. The battery in my watch died, so I no longer had indicators of time or pace. This led to another surreal stretch of time. Without anything to measure, a handful of minutes seemed like an hour. My feet blistered. The blisters I had before that day now had children and grandchildren. No longer was there a way to walk without pain in each step.

As sunset approached, the aid stations offered cups of chicken broth. After 15 hours of sweet foods and drinks, that was the ambrosia of life. When the volunteer, who was about 12, handed me my first cup he said sarcastically, "It is *totally* homemade." As the saltiness of the broth passed my lips, I thought it was one of the best things that I ever consumed. I don't care if there were boxes of generic chicken broth on the ground — *THAT* — tasted homemade.

I meandered along the path with the thought that I had tons of time. I just needed to keep moving. The truth was, I was fine on time... until suddenly I wasn't.

I passed an aid station about a mile and a half from the turnaround point. The volunteer urged everyone to, "GO!" As in, I had less than 20 minutes until my race would be over, unless I could pick up the pace.

I did my best to ignore the shooting pain with every footfall. About a mile later, I was on the edge of the lake. I could see the turn in the distance, it seemed impossibly far away although it was less than a quarter mile. A volunteer was there, emphatically giving time splits, I had six minutes to make it to the timing mat. I pushed hard and crossed the timing mat with less than two minutes to cut-off.

Several minutes later, I saw people still trying their hardest to make it to the cut-off, but I was sure that their race was over. Less than six miles to the end of a 140.6-mile race and they came up short. I forced myself not to feel what they must have felt. I kept my head down and shuffled forward.

Periodically, there was a road construction light on the trail. From a distance, it was a lighthouse piercing the darkness, to illuminate the path. At first, it seemed like a trick of my eyes, a mirage of the night. Is there really a light ahead, or is it a vision of what I hoped to see? Then it would take shape and get brighter and brighter. As I got closer, it became blinding. Then, once the light was to my back, it projected a shadow of my battered and broken self into the distance. As I continued onward, my walk-shuffle turned into a shuffle-limp.

I kept up with a racer on the course, until she saw her boyfriend and her pace picked up. I slowly faded back. I was alone, again.

I started composing the social media message I would send out in the next few hours, "I did my best, but it just wasn't my day." Tears streamed down my face as I tried to find a way to spin it as anything other than a painful, expensive, waste of time. Afterall, my friends and family would understand and be supportive. Even worse, an email went out at work and all my colleagues, company-wide, knew I was racing today. It would be especially tough going into work and explaining my failure to people who didn't understand why I did this.

At that moment, I forgot my "why". I was just openly weeping and walking along a forest trail. I wanted to reach the finish line, not for the sense of accomplishment, but so I could simply stop. Stop walking, stop hurting, stop feeling alone. Just stop.

From the darkness, I heard familiar voices. I dried my eyes and listened closely. I desperately hoped that it wasn't a mind game — just me hearing what I wanted to hear.

Seeing my friends meant more to me than I could ever express. They came to give whatever encouragement I needed to get to the finish line. They gave me strength to continue.

At 50 yards to go, I stopped for a moment and gave the racer in front of me a chance to go in on her own. I pulled down my top (Picard maneuver) and entered the finishing chute. The floodlights bathed the carpet in the final yards of the course. Moments ago, I was physically in the dark and then I was under blinding lights. The crowd screamed encouragement louder than anything I've ever heard.

I gave a high-five to every outstretched hand I could, there were 100s of them. I felt like a rock star on the largest stage in the planet. I made my way to give my wife a kiss prior to crossing the finish line. She was surrounded by my closest friends — they were all sobbing.

I made my way towards the finish line and realized that four magical words would signify the end of my journey. I didn't hear them over the noise of the crowd. I resigned to the fact that I would have to re-watch the finish online, to hear. I crossed the finish line to a mob of people. I had friends who volunteered the last shift of the race to be there to "catch" me as I crossed and present me my medal. I received a medal and hugs from good friends, when the race director took my arm, "What's your name again?"

I was flooded with panic and thought I was in trouble, "Scott" I answered. He led me back to the carpet.

He spoke to the crowd, through the microphone, "Scott here, is one of our last finishers tonight...Scott the people here have something they want to tell you...YOU..."

The crowd of 100s, which felt like 5000, spoke in unison:

"ARE AN IRONMAN!!!"

My knees nearly buckled. The four words I was waiting to hear.

I re-crossed the finish line, and I let out a primal scream of celebration.

At that point I became suddenly aware of the still and video cameras pointed at me. I thought to myself, "Oh please, please, please, don't ask me a question or try to interview me. I won't be able to keep it together."

I completed my race in 17 hours. I finished in last place — with less than four minutes to cut-off.

Now, the pages have emerged for a new chapter in my story. I will be racing for Team USA in September 2020, in the Aquabike World Championships.

"It's not what you achieve that makes you who you are. Who you are makes you what you can achieve."

~Valerie A. Haller

Authors' Biographies

tommyzphotos.com

Katie Zaferes is the 2019 ITU World Champion and a 2016 Olympian. She is married to Tommy Zaferes and the two get to travel the world together while racing and training for triathlon. Follow Katie on Twitter @kzaferes6

Thomas Haller is an internationally recognized presenter, an award-winning author of nine highly acclaimed books, a psychotherapist maintaining a 32-year private practice as a child, adolescent, and couple's therapist, and the CEO of an Independent Publishing company — Personal Power Press, Inc. For inspiring presentations on getting the best out of yourself, raising responsible children, or creating a compassionate marriage. Contact Thomas at thomas@thomashaller.com or visit his website at www.thomashaller.com

Valerie Haller is an Early Childhood Specialist with a master's degree in education. She has taught kindergarten in the public schools for thirty-two years. She started competing in triathlons ten years ago for something to do during summer break. Valerie is a breast cancer survivor and the founder of ValhallaTRI Club for Kids. A safe place for kids to learn about triathlon and practice their swim, bike, and run skills. Contact Valerie at vahaller@hotmail.com or visit www.valhallatri.com.

Photo by Wendy
Andrews

Lauren Jensen McGinnis is a Professional Triathlon Coach and Motivational Speaker from Muskego, Wisconsin. She combines her knowledge as a Physical Therapist with over 30 years of coaching experience, making her one of the premier Triathlon Coaches in the country. As the owner and Head Coach of Tri Faster, Lauren makes it her mission to help athletes achieve goals beyond what they initially feel is possible. Contact Coach Lauren at 414-430-2467 or email lauren.shark.jensen@gmail.

Edward Marx is passionate about God, Simran, Kids, Tango, and Triathlon serving on a mission to transform healthcare. For more information visit www.marxconsult.com.

Sybille Rex is a competitive age group triathlete, wife, mom, Ambassador for the USAT Foundation, and current member of Team USA. Professionally, she is a USAT certified triathlon coach and owner of "REX Multisport Coaching", swim instructor at LifeTime Fitness, USMS Swim Coach, and Spin/Group Fitness Instructor whose mission is to "Help others lead a healthy life through fitness and chase their athletic dreams". Contact Sybille at sybrex@hotmail.com or visit https://www.facebook.com/Triathlete.SybilleRex/ or https://www.facebook.com/REX.Multisport.Coaching/.

Shay Eskew is an All American / IRONMAN®, All World ranked triathlete, Healthcare RCM strategist, former black bear researcher, burn survivor with scars over 65% of his body, motivational speaker and best-selling author of "What the Fire Ignited". Contact Shay at inspire@shayeskew.com or visit his website at www.shayeskew.com.

Christie Petersen with a gritty, positive, never give up attitude, I have been able to accomplish many things in life. I listen to my heart and soul, not those who doubt me. I hope my story inspires you to do great things. Contact Christie at cp.christie.petersen@gmail.com.

Jen Klouse is originally from Millington, Michigan and currently resides in a suburb of Chicago, Illinois. She graduated from Central Michigan University with a Bachelor of Science in Psychology and a minor in Art. Besides athletics, helping people and her faith, she's passionate about art and traveling the world. Her hope is that her story will influence at least one person in this world to make the decision to become an organ donor. Contact Jen at klouse54@gmail.com.

Kathy Kleinert was born and raised in Bay City, Michigan, and currently resides in Sanford, Michigan with her husband. She has a degree from a local university and works in a science and toxicology field. Her hobbies include triathlons, photography, reading, kayaking, fishing, hiking and camping. Contact Kathy at kathykleinert@yahoo.com.

Joe McCarthy is a three-time Paralympic swimmer, a keynote speaker, insurance sales professional and triathlete. Joe is passionate about helping people move forward from trauma. Joe has provided more than 50 keynote speeches to large and small companies alike. For speaking engagements, contact Joe directly at josephmccarthy@yahoo.com.

Tim Wilkinson is an endurance junkie who seeks out the long races that will challenge him. Contact Tim at Facebook -
https://www.facebook.com/tim.wilkinson.10
Instagram - sirsufferkingkos, Twitter - SirTimWilkinson

Photo from www.bob–haller.eu

Bob Haller is a Multiple National Champion and Professional Triathlete from Imbringen, Luxembourg with an International Triathlon Union (ITU) world ranking of 70. Contact Bob at www.bob-haller.eu or www.twitter.com/bobh_triathlete.

Tenchi So is a former martial artist and a Fast-Twitch Anaerobic Explosive Athlete in a Slow-Twitch Aerobic World. Tenchi So, IRONMAN® and Traveling Triathlete. Contact Tenchi at tenchiso@aim.com.

Scott Baranek is a certified Prosthetist from both BOC and ABC. He has dedicated his career to providing high end prosthetic care and creating resources which improve ambulatory rehabilitation for amputees in the Tri-City community. For more information visit www.bremerprosthetics.com.

Maggie Rettelle is a dedicated to being the best mother, daughter, partner and friend to those in her life. Maggie is a passionate Registered Dietitian, coach and accomplished age group triathlete and marathoner that loves to share her knowledge and insight to inspire others to be their best. Contact Maggie at MaggieRettelle.fit@gmail.com.

Michael Ducharme is a Heroes Ambassador for St. Jude Children's Research Hospital, raising over $30,000 since 2015. For questions on becoming a St. Jude Hero, or to donate, contact Michael at stjudemike@gmail.com.

Frank Szostak is a 54-year-old father of two, and a resident of Michigan. His triathlete journey began in 2012, and with the loving support of his best half Jamie, he continues to reach for new goals in this sport that he loves. Contact Frank at fw_smith2000@yahoo.com.

Branden Scheel has been a triathlete for 13 years, racing with some of the world's best the last few years. It has allowed him to travel the world and meet his wife-to-be! He also loves coaching athletes of all abilities. Contact Branden at branden.scheel@aol.com.

Jennifer Brown lives in Saginaw, Michigan. She is a dedicated wife, boy mom, marathoner, and triathlete. Contact Jennifer at jenbrown10@gmail.com.

Brandon McDonald is a Triathlete from Fremont, Michigan. I don't believe in limits, with God anything is possible. Love, live and inspire! Contact Brandon at brandonmcdonald15075@yahoo.com Instagram @lovesurfrun.

Donna Heska has Bachelor of Business Administration/Registered Respiratory Therapist, Senior Clinical Sales Specialist, Bayer Healthcare. Optimism, Perseverance, Goals, & Dreams Lead to the Achievement of SUCCESS!!! Two-time ITU World Qualification, Gold Coast Australia, 2018 & Lausanne Switzerland, 2019. Contact Donna at donnaheska@charter.net.

Betty Bustrum is 70 years old, blessed to be the mother of three children and 10 grandchildren. She has been competing in the sport of triathlon for 17 years and hopes to continue for years to come! Contact Betty at cyclebab@yahoo.com.

Roseann Peiffer lives and trains in Maumee, Ohio with her husband and dog Luna. Contact Roseann at: rperchi87@gmail.com.

Jennifer Weber is a fitness enthusiast, 4-time IRONMAN® athlete, and life coach for WebMD Health Services for over 13 years and is also the regional leader for FiA (Females in Action) in Jacksonville, Florida. Her passion to help others develop healthy lifestyles is exemplified in her professional and personal life. Utilizing her experience and education she creates motivational programs in health and fitness to increase awareness and promote healthier lifestyles. To contact Jennifer at JenniferMW83@gmail.com.

Scott Gayler and his wife of 25 years have been members of the Seattle Green Lake Triathlon Group (http://sgltg.org) for the past five years. He has lost nearly 100 pounds in preparation for the Aquabike World Championships in Almere, Netherlands in September of 2020. Contact Scott at scottgyler@gmail.com.

About the Author

Most people know Valerie Haller as Ms. Val, a kindergarten teacher who has whispered to the spirit of children, as a public-school teacher for 32 years. Those who have had the opportunity to be in the classroom with Ms. Val experience a peaceful learning environment — where there is a song for everything and a place for everyone.

Ten years ago, an unsettling feeling crept into Valerie's kindergarten bubble, an emptiness deep inside began to take root. The songs in her heart quieted and her passion waned. She pondered, perhaps it was just the long Michigan winter or the increased independence of her two boys who seemed to need her motherly touch less and less. She knew that something needed to change to regain her kindergarten muse.

Home alone one cold winter evening, she received a call from a friend who invited her to a new exercise class at the local college. She joined the class that evening to support her friend not knowing where it would lead. The Pilates instructor took note of her persistent energy and invited her to a spin class the following evening. Two nights a week, either spinning or Pilates over a couple of months, blossomed into running on the treadmill another evening or two. One evening after spin class, Valerie stopped by the aerobics room for a brief treadmill run. She climbed aboard a machine and started jogging.

After several minutes the man on the treadmill next to her inquired, "Didn't I just see you in the spin class? Are you a triathlete?"

"No, just a kindergarten teacher," she replied.

"Well, it sure looks like you could be," the man commented as he stepped off his machine. "Have a good workout."

"Triathlete" struck a chord deep inside. It was never a term she used to describe herself before. As she contemplated the possibility —

an unfamiliar feeling came over her — a desire to win. She felt her legs begin to glide effortlessly over the treadmill, and the emptiness she was feeling began to subside. A competitive spirit filled her, and she felt alive once again. That was the moment a kindergarten teacher turned into a triathlete.

To this day, Valerie has competed in over 40 triathlons. The first years were about finishing, but that soon subsided, and the competitive spirit pushed her to first place in her age group, and then first or second overall. Valerie competed in the USA Triathlon Nationals for four years and was a member of Team USA, competing in the Triathlon World Championships 2018, in Gold Coast, Australia.

A month after returning from Australia, Valerie was diagnosed with breast cancer. That is where her story began, in *TRIing Times*.